The
Fender
Stratocaster
Handbook

First published in 2007 by MBI Publishing Company LLC and Voyageur Press, an imprint of MBI Publishing Company, Galtier Plaza, Suite 200, 380 Jackson Street, St. Paul, MN 55101-3885 USA

MBI Publishing Company titles are also available at discounts in bulk quantity for industrial or sales-promotional use. For details write to Special Sales Manager at MBI Publishing Company, Galtier Plaza, Suite 200, 380 Jackson Street, St. Paul, MN 55101-3885 USA.

ISBN-13: 978-0-7603-2983-2

ISBN-10: 0-7603-2983-4

Printed in England

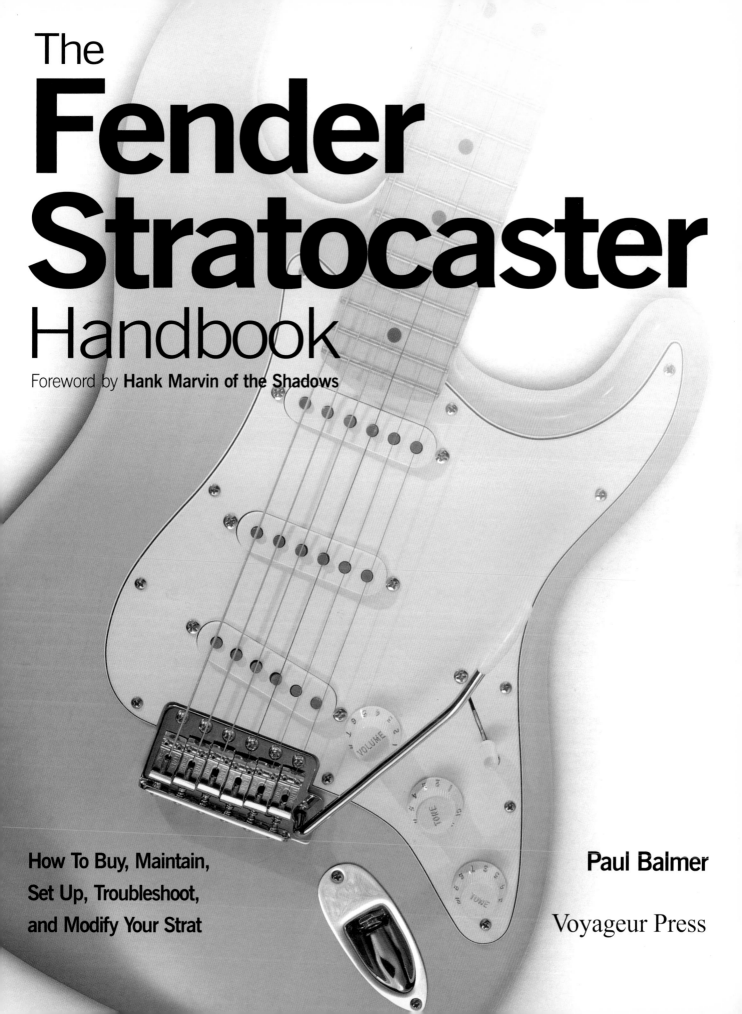

The Fender Stratocaster Handbook

Foreword by **Hank Marvin of the Shadows**

How To Buy, Maintain,
Set Up, Troubleshoot,
and Modify Your Strat

Paul Balmer

Voyageur Press

Contents

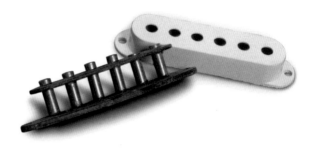

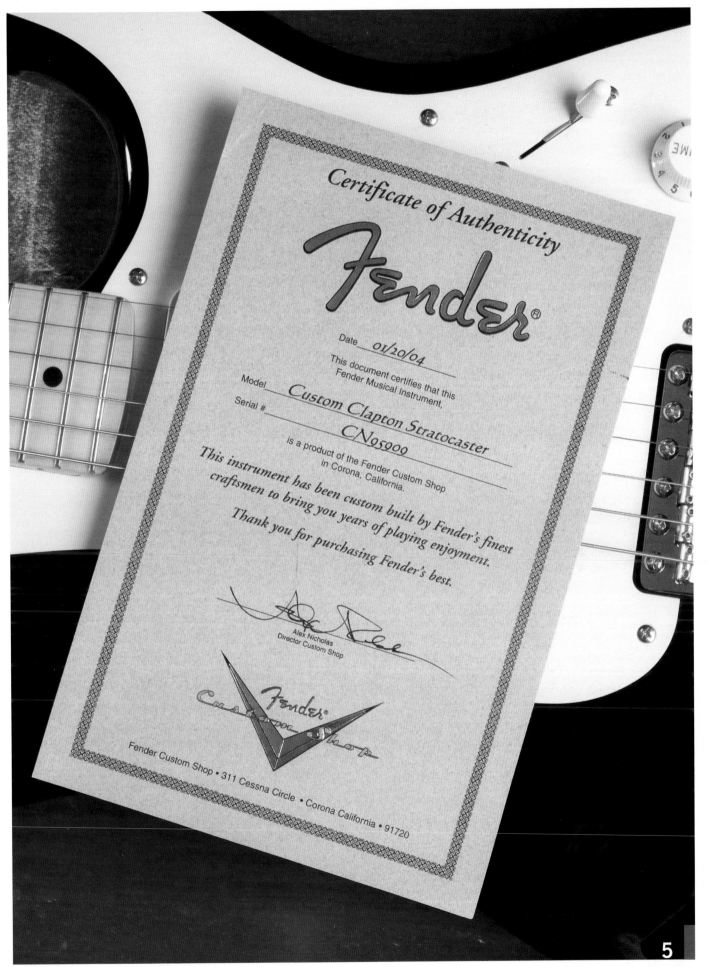

Certificate of Authenticity

Fender®

Date __01/20/04__

This document certifies that this
Fender Musical Instrument,

Model __Custom Clapton Stratocaster__

Serial # __CN95909__

is a product of the Fender Custom Shop
in Corona, California.

This instrument has been custom built by Fender's finest
craftsmen to bring you years of playing enjoyment.

Thank you for purchasing Fender's best.

Alex Nicholas
Director Custom Shop

Fender® Custom Shop

Fender Custom Shop • 311 Cessna Circle • Corona California • 91720

5

Foreword by Hank Marvin

Hank Marvin had a huge influence on guitarists such as Brian May of Queen, Mark Knopfler of Dire Straits and George Harrison of The Beatles. Through Hank, hundreds of other players were introduced to the potential of the Fender Stratocaster. His phrasing and dynamics are legendary, and he remains a great musician, now suitably honoured with his own 'Signature' Strat.

The first time I saw a real live Strat was in 1959 when the guitar that Cliff Richard had ordered for me arrived from the Fender factory in the USA.

We pulled the flat 'tweed' guitar case out of the packaging box and with fumbling fingers I slowly undid the three catches and opened the case. There it lay, almost unreal, more beautiful than the photographs. A Fender Stratocaster with a Bird's Eye Maple neck, attached to a red body with a white pick guard sporting not two, but three pick ups! The effect was further enhanced by gold-plated hardware and a revolutionary tremolo arm.

The Strat was lightweight and, because of the contoured body, with no hard edges, very comfortable to hold and play. The strings on my first Strat were heavy, 13-56, but what a sound; like a piano.

The possibilities of the vibrato bar intrigued me. I started to experiment with holding the bar in the palm of my right hand as I picked the strings: this became part of my Strat technique and enabled me to produce a vibrato on the heavy strings. Finger vibrato 'blues style' was not something we were aware of back then, although I had heard Django Reinhardt recordings and he used a wonderful natural vibrato. My vibrato technique helps the guitar sustain, and I still use it even with comparatively lighter strings (currently 11-50).

Using the bar I was able to add various ornamentation effects, such as 'bending' a note down, or starting under pitch and 'bending' up to the target note, giving a dramatic or frenzied 'shake', and it also helped me bend the heavy 1st and 2nd strings.

The guitar I was using prior to that Strat had a neck that could have been made by Fred Flintstone: it was thick and bent, producing an action that was almost painful over the 5th to 10th frets. In contrast the Strat had a beautiful neck and fingerboard and was a joy to play.

The first recording using the Strat was on Cliff's second album. By that time I had my Vox (Meazzi) Echo Box (similiar to that illustrated), a Vox AC 30 amp and my sound and style was beginning to take shape. A sound and style that would not have developed with any other guitar but the Stratocaster. Leo, I am forever grateful.

Speaking from experience, a badly set up guitar can suck all of the joy out of your playing, so to get the best out of your Strat and enjoyment to the max, you need to have it set up correctly. A qualified guitar tech/repairman will be able to do this for you, or perhaps you could try this manual?

The relief on the neck can be adjusted along with the bridge height so that a good buzz-free action can be achieved, the floating bridge can be set up so that any tuning problems associated with use of the vibrato bar are virtually eliminated. The intonation can also be fine-tuned by adjustment of the individual bridge saddles. If you are not delighted and inspired by the difference, sell the guitar and take up flower arranging.

Yes, the ubiquitous Fender Stratocaster is a remarkable instrument, not only because of its sensuous and much-copied appearance, but also in its numerous practical innovations and versatility, capable of producing a wide variety of sounds. That's why it is the instrument of choice for so many stylistically diverse guitarists.

Although at times I strayed and had brief dalliances with other electric guitars, these only served to confirm what I already knew in my heart: I would always return to my 'Strat' – she was, and is, the one.

September 2006

Introduction

Leo Fender was a genius. He couldn't play guitar, but he talked to those who could and understood their problems as working musicians. He gave them a set of solutions, which created a revolutionary new instrument, the working man's electric Spanish guitar. There were those that scoffed at Leo's audacity, his blatantly sexy 'electric plank', but 50 odd years later it's a revered classic.

There had been attempts to make electric guitars before 1954 and they satisfied some players. But the 'electric guitar' was still a poor cousin and the term 'electric' a derogatory generic 'put down'. Real musicians still played the 'pure' acoustic guitar.

Leo himself had started a radical shift with his 1950 'Broadcaster' and 1951 'Precision' bass. But with the Stratocaster Leo and his team brought a practical inventor's genius to the table and created an icon of the 20th century.

When Leo and his colleagues designed the Stratocaster they were immersed in the first flush of the post Second World War space age – literally reaching beyond 'telecasting' and aiming for the stratosphere (located a significant 'eight miles high'). With a name attributed to Don Randall and probably inspired by the Boeing B-52 'Stratofortress' of 1954, they were 'Stratocasting' 20 years before Concorde entered the stratosphere.

In the first year of manufacture, however, Leo and his intrepid pioneers faced outright ridicule. They only sold 700 guitars and the instrument became widely regarded as a joke – a flash in the pan. Now the Stratocaster is the embodiment of the generic image of the electric guitar. In 1964 Leo sold his business for $13 million, quite a respectable sum for a company that was initially ridiculed by other manufacturers for selling a 'canoe paddle with strings'.

It's been great fun examining the science of Leo's masterwork for this manual. However, the genius of the Stratocaster is that rare blend of art and science that creates sheer magic. Every time I glanced at the guitar for a measurement or technical detail all I really wanted to do was play it! The Strat is a magnetic siren. They come in blonde, brunette and fiery red, and remain untamed after more than 50 years of carousing abuse.

Enjoy giving your Strat a 'tune up' but then put down your Allen key and wail.

I was always able to see the defects in the design of an instrument which overlooked completely the need of its maintenance. If something is easy to repair, it is easy to construct. The design of each element should be thought out in order to be easy to make and easy to repair.

Leo Fender

A Classic Strat

Shown much as it appeared in 1954, the then radical guitar breaks down into approximately 150 discreet components – all originally conceived as easily replaceable.

Alchemy results in the whole becoming much more than the sum of the parts. The parts are interesting however, if only for how much Leo Fender and his team were correct about in this updated 'Fender guitar'.

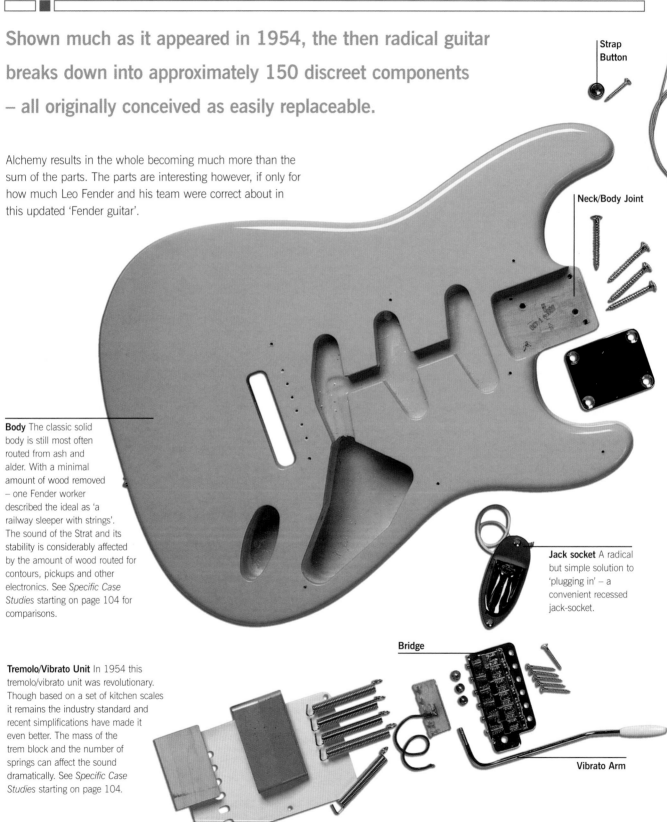

Strap Button

Neck/Body Joint

Body The classic solid body is still most often routed from ash and alder. With a minimal amount of wood removed – one Fender worker described the ideal as 'a railway sleeper with strings'. The sound of the Strat and its stability is considerably affected by the amount of wood routed for contours, pickups and other electronics. See *Specific Case Studies* starting on page 104 for comparisons.

Jack socket A radical but simple solution to 'plugging in' – a convenient recessed jack-socket.

Bridge

Tremolo/Vibrato Unit In 1954 this tremolo/vibrato unit was revolutionary. Though based on a set of kitchen scales it remains the industry standard and recent simplifications have made it even better. The mass of the trem block and the number of springs can affect the sound dramatically. See *Specific Case Studies* starting on page 104.

Vibrato Arm

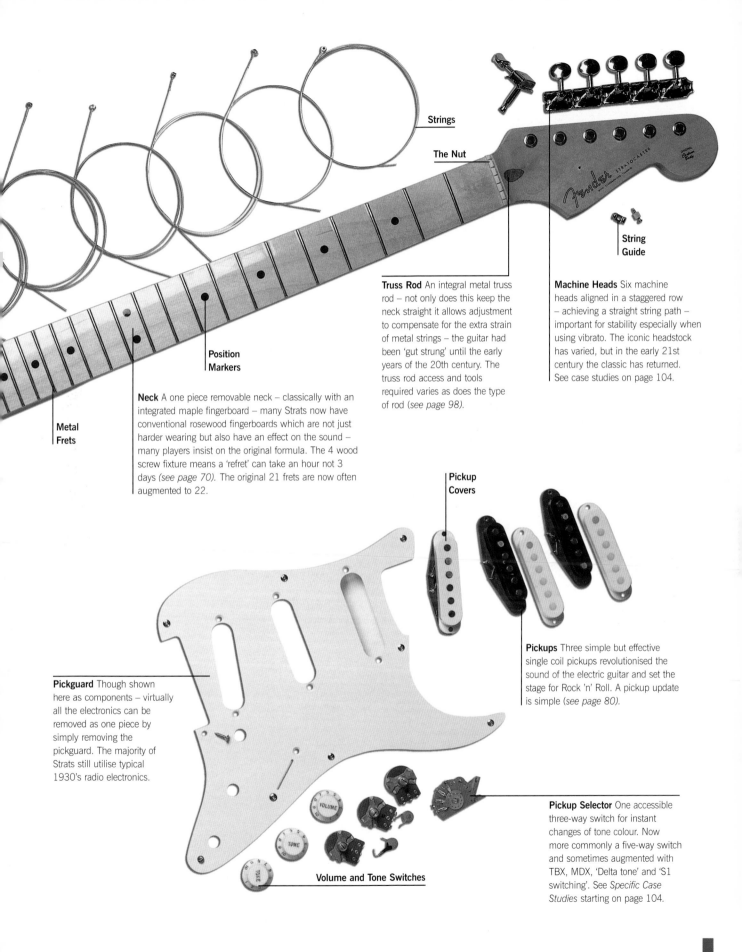

Strings

The Nut

String Guide

Truss Rod An integral metal truss rod – not only does this keep the neck straight it allows adjustment to compensate for the extra strain of metal strings – the guitar had been 'gut strung' until the early years of the 20th century. The truss rod access and tools required varies as does the type of rod (*see page 98*).

Machine Heads Six machine heads aligned in a staggered row – achieving a straight string path – important for stability especially when using vibrato. The iconic headstock has varied, but in the early 21st century the classic has returned. See case studies on page 104.

Position Markers

Metal Frets

Neck A one piece removable neck – classically with an integrated maple fingerboard – many Strats now have conventional rosewood fingerboards which are not just harder wearing but also have an effect on the sound – many players insist on the original formula. The 4 wood screw fixture means a 'refret' can take an hour not 3 days (*see page 70*). The original 21 frets are now often augmented to 22.

Pickup Covers

Pickups Three simple but effective single coil pickups revolutionised the sound of the electric guitar and set the stage for Rock 'n' Roll. A pickup update is simple (*see page 80*).

Pickguard Though shown here as components – virtually all the electronics can be removed as one piece by simply removing the pickguard. The majority of Strats still utilise typical 1930's radio electronics.

Pickup Selector One accessible three-way switch for instant changes of tone colour. Now more commonly a five-way switch and sometimes augmented with TBX, MDX, 'Delta tone' and 'S1 switching'. See *Specific Case Studies* starting on page 104.

Volume and Tone Switches

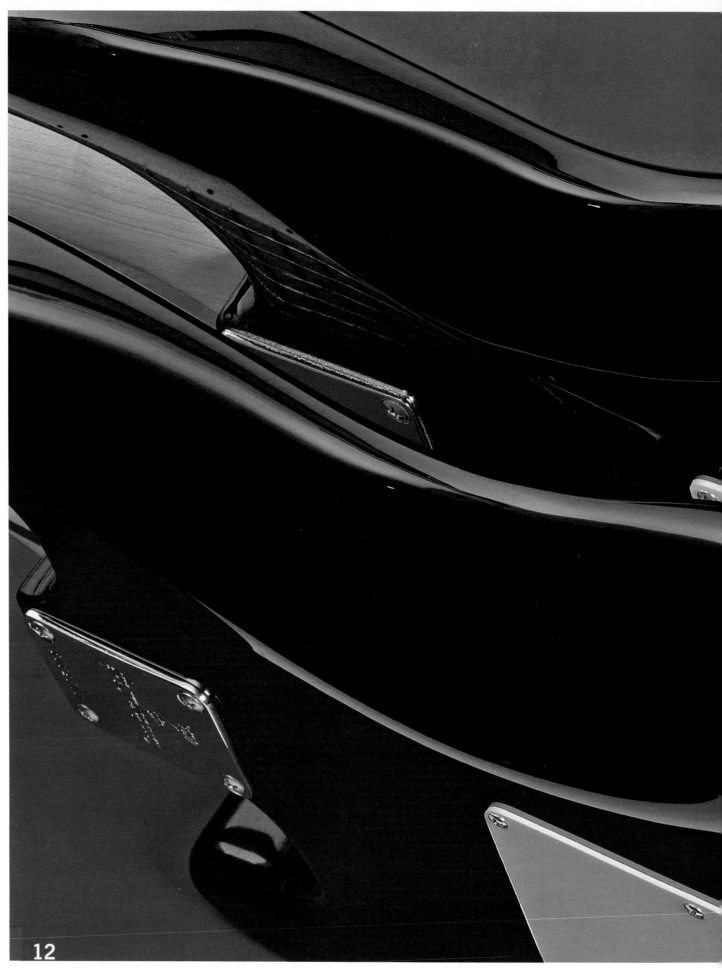

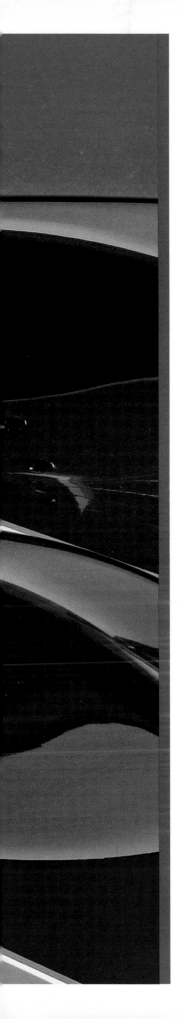

Buying a Stratocaster

Just as with many cars these days the Fender Stratocaster comes in many styles and with several 'optional extras'. All Strats share a common essential body outline, but as you might expect there are considerable differences between the budget 'Indonesian or Japanese made' Squier and a top-of-the-line 'Eric Clapton' custom shop limited edition.

There are also, of course, many 'previously loved' options, from an original 1954 Sunburst, which may require a second mortgage to finance, to a second-hand Squier bought at a car boot sale for $60. Leo Fender's classic 'working man's' guitar has spawned a plethora of 'Horses for courses'.

LEFT An Eric Clapton custom shop 'Blackie' and a Chinese Squier.

RIGHT Eric Clapton custom shop guitar.

■ Fender Squier Stratocasters

Made at different times in Korea, Indonesia, Japan and Mexico, these will delight any student. They look like a classic Strat, sound very similar, and when well 'set up' can perform well enough to satisfy the most discerning ear. I've even seen professional session musicians playing Squiers and making them sound as good as any guitar you are ever likely to hear. Bear in mind, however, that these musicians have probably done a bit of 'hot rodding' – changing the pickups and having the neck and bridge professionally aligned.

There is no standard Squier but rather a range of very affordable options, with different pickup configurations and other variants. There are even 'kit ' versions at present which offer the novice everything to get started, including amp, pick, and guitar lead.

■ The American 'Series' (previously American Standard)

Introduced in 1986, this is Fender's benchmark Strat. Still current in 2006, with 'Made In the USA' proudly emblazoned about its person, this is the real deal. Leo's original concept remains largely intact with some minor 'improvements'. These vary each year but generally include:

A Fender Squier Stratocaster.   An American 'Series' Stratocaster.

1. A headstock end truss rod adjustment, which is much easier to access than the 'classic' neck heal version.

2. A redesigned set of bridge saddles, with more mass and less susceptibility to corrosion. This produces a slightly different sound characteristic that some players may prefer.

3. A five-way selector switch, fitted as standard from 1977 onwards and offering all the classic pickup combinations without resort to matchsticks.

4. Modern 'eco friendly' paint finishes. Note, however, that the non-eco friendly versions are still available in the Vintage series. There are theories that the paint finish can affect the sound of a solid guitar – the old finishes allowed the wood to 'breathe', whereas newer paint options, whilst kinder to the environment, form an airtight seal on the solid guitar body, preventing further drying and seasoning.

5. Modern machine heads and other hardware – see *Know your American Series Strat* on page 24 for more on this.

6. Pickup options. These days you can choose from classic pickup designs, 'noiseless' versions (stacked humbuckers), classic humbuckers, and versions with associated active electronics. They all sound subtly different and you select either the choice of your heroes or whatever combination suits your own personal identity. The prices vary immensely,depending on the particular options you choose.

2 Other Strat options in 2006

■ Vintage Reissues

This series offers new American guitars very much in the mould of Leo Fender's original classics. The 'settled' Strat of 1957, incorporating custom colours and a maple fingerboard, is offered alongside a classic 1962 with a rosewood board. These come complete with vintage tweed cases and accessories. They can be brilliant guitars, incorporating as they do all the classic features but with a consistency of production only dreamed of in 1954. See *Case Study '57 Reissue* on page 110.

■ Custom Shop

You ask for the pickups and other details you want and get them! A bewildering range of Strats for all tastes.

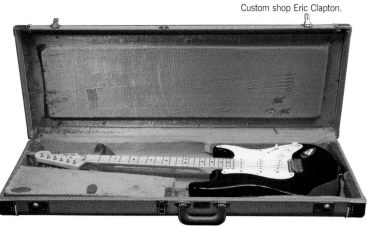

Custom shop Eric Clapton.

■ Relics

A fascinating area. True vintage guitars were becoming unaffordable for the average player, and this is Fender's response. You can currently purchase a 'relic' Strat which, though newly manufactured, has been artificially distressed to emulate the appearance and character of a '50s, '60s or '70s original.

■ Closet Classics

A new but relatively lightly distressed classic which is meant to simulate a guitar kept in a closet for 40–50 years! See *Case Study '54 Reissue* on page 106.

Closet Classic '54.

■ N.O.S.

You can also purchase 'N.O.S.', New Old Stock, a new guitar as if made from materials in the year of original manufacture and brought to the present in a time machine!

■ Signature Series Strats

As you would expect, these bear the signature of Hank Marvin, Jeff Beck and others and are very similar to the Strat designed and sometimes played by the signatory. Be aware, however, that celebrity players have vast collections of guitars and may play any number of them for recordings and gigs. See *Case Study 'Eric Clapton'* on page 128.

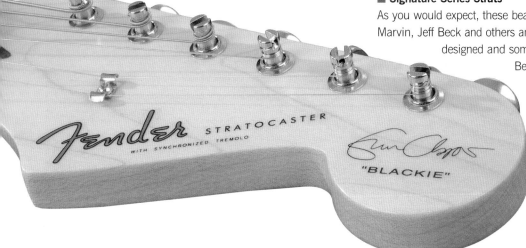

Buy from a reputable dealer who will be there next year when you need a repair or replacement, someone who you trust and can give advice on strings and other peripherals. The music industry has many trade associations and members will display their membership in the shop: look out for that – it's your guarantee of the minimum standard of service you should expect.

Buy from a private seller only if you know your way around the guitar and know precisely what you want. Never buy in the proverbial back street from an untraceable source.

Remember that all Strat parts are still currently available in 2006 and, it seems likely, will remain so for the forseeable future. What you are buying is a design classic.

Some issues to address when buying second-hand

■ Corrosion of metal parts

Some parts of the guitar in frequent contact with sweaty palms will tend to corrode over the years. The most common area is the bridge. This is generally not serious. (See page 53 for more on corrosion issues).

■ Fret wear

An old, well-played guitar may need re-fretting. This is not often a major issue. Seek advice and a price from an expert. Your dealer may give you a discount if you negotiate the re-fret with his in-house technicians. (See page 149 for more on fretting issues).

■ Fingerboard wear

This may also be an issue, particularly on maple necks. However, even bad wear can be 'in-filled'. You must weigh up the options based on how much you're attracted to the individual instrument. A new neck is an option, though a Fender one can be pricey – you may consider an equivalent replacement. However, please avoid disassembling a rare vintage instrument if at all possible.

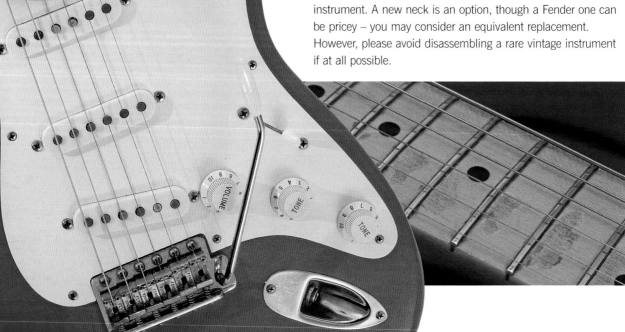

■ Machine heads

These can be replaced (*see page 38*).

■ Pickups

Are they all working? Broken covers can easily be replaced.

■ Noisy tone and volume controls and switches

These can either be cleaned or replaced (*see page 85*).

■ Missing parts

Tremolo arms, plastic knobs and 'ashtrays' (chrome bridge covers) are frequently missing – they are easily replaced. Strive to replace these with appropriate, even 'vintage' repro, parts.

■ Authenticity

Buyers must beware when buying a supposedly 'vintage' guitar. Fender mark their Vintage Reissue and Relic guitars clearly. However, as a 1954 Fender Strat is currently selling for $25,000 plus, with one knob being worth $500, unscrupulous individuals may try to pass of a relatively inexpensive reissue as the priceless real thing. Serial numbers can be a useful guide (*see appendix*). However, even they can be faked. Only the most experienced expert can distinguish the telltale distinctions of paint finish, wear and tear, wiring details, etc, which distinguish the real thing.

If it were a car you might call an automobile association for a roadside check, so for a vintage guitar why not get a guitar tech to do just that? Most reputable dealers can recommend a technician with specialist knowledge of Fenders. An expert guitar tech will rely as much on 'feel' in making an assessment as an antiques dealer would in assessing a piece of furniture.

In the end vintage guitars are wonderful artefacts and historical icons, but good music comes from the player's imagination and musicality as much *if not more* than any other factor. Eric Clapton, for instance, is most frequently seen playing brand new Strats – he saves the vintage ones for recording! Vintage guitars are in fact less useful on stage these days as they are naturally more prone to electrical interference from the sophisticated lighting rigs which were rare in 1954.

Verifying authenticity

It may seem sacrosanct to disassemble a supposed vintage instrument. However, the telltale details of vintage wiring and even solder types can mark the real thing from a reproduction. Cloth shielding on pickup wiring is a useful clue to early Fenders, but the unscrupulous will borrow such wiring from an old radio.

Laboratory paint analysis will reveal such clues as early nitrocellulose lacquer rather than modern polyurethanes. Fender used 100 per cent nitrocellulose paints until 1969 and the colours were strictly limited. After 1969 Strats had a catalysed undercoat and lacquer topcoat. The undercoat is often revealed in the crudely routed pickup cavities of early guitars.

Seek provenance, just like an auction house such as Sotheby's or Christies would – this might include original sales documentation, hang tags, original cases, photographs of the instrument in use in a dateable form, etc.

The irony of all the chicanery of fraudsters is that it is perfectly possible now to buy a new Stratocaster that plays better, and to my ears sometimes even sounds better, than a vintage gem. This doesn't devalue the beauty and grace of Leo's original concept one iota – in fact it supports Leo's original concept of a 'working man's' guitar: in tune, sounding great, and affordable.

I personally prefer my Vintage Reissue '57 to my first real guitar, a 1963 Fiesta Red. All the manufacturing tolerances seem more accurate on the new one. Fender now has much more sophisticated computer regulated machining and as a result the new guitar *stays in tune*, which the vintage one sadly never did.

Know your Vintage Strat

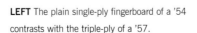

The 'classic' Fender Stratocaster breaks down into approximately 150 pieces. This perfectly illustrates Leo Fender's original concept of a 'parts assembled' guitar, consistent in quality and with every component easily replaceable.

LEFT The plain single-ply fingerboard of a '54 contrasts with the triple-ply of a '57.

RIGHT A fine '54 custom shop limited edition by John Cruz.

■ Frets

Originally the guitar featured 21 frets giving a top C#. This seemingly odd choice reflects the guitar's 'home key' of E, which has C# as it's sixth. I suspect Leo was thinking 'B' and then going the extra mile (or up to 'eleven', as Spinal Tap would eventually see it). Subsequent Fenders have an added 22nd fret, giving a top D the minor 7th in key of E.

■ Maple neck

A feature of the original concept was Leo Fender's one-piece 'disposable' neck. Many early 20th-century guitars had warped necks due to the 'new' strain of metal strings. Prior to 1920 most guitars were strung with much lower tension 'gut' strings.

■ Nut

The relatively narrow nut was regarded as an aid to easy playing in the days before players evolved advanced string-bending techniques.

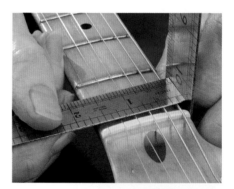

■ Double cutaways

These were another innovation. They enable easy access to what guitarist Martin Taylor refers to as 'the dusty end of the fingerboard'. Fender guitarists soon exploited the top octave of the guitar, which had been previously difficult to access and largely neglected – one way in which Leo's invention radically changed popular music.

■ Body contours

The Stratocaster was seen by Leo as an improvement on his previous Broadcaster/Telecaster design. One notable innovation was the body contouring. Several players had complained that with Leo's previous guitar designs, such as the Telecaster, the simple slab body could dig into your chest during a long session. Leo's response was outrageous, pragmatic, simple, and effective. Consequently many early Stratocasters have very severe experimental contouring. We now take such features totally for granted.

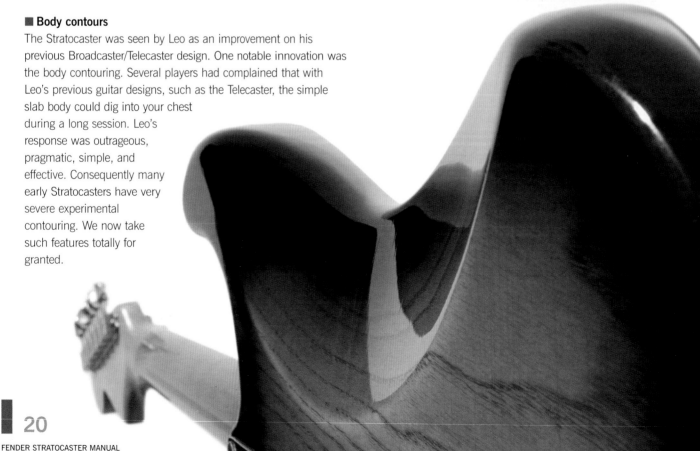

ABOVE Rounded pickup covers and truss rod access.

■ Truss rod

Leo was amongst the first to adopt a relatively accessible adjustable metal truss rod in order to rectify neck-warping problems. His radical thinking also embraced the concept of 'throwaway' replaceable necks.

 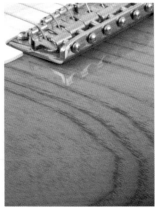

■ Position Markers

Traditional Spanish guitars have no position marker 'dots', but with the new access to the higher positions afforded on the Strat such visual clues were very welcome.

■ Body

Made of Ash until 1956 when Leo switched to Alder. Each wood has a subtly different effect on the acoustic sound of the Strat and this carries over to the amplified sound. Leo preferred Ash to Alder but Ash was occasionally prone to a disfiguring 'raised' grain. The body is not always 'one-piece'. and although many '50s Strats are one-piece, Leo never insisted on this.

■ Tremolo/Vibrato

One of the items that changed the sound of popular music. This was not the first 'vibrato' device, but was the first that worked without causing intonation problems.

The deceptively simple mechanics of the 'balanced fulcrum' were in fact Leo's second attempt. His perfectionism meant he scrapped hundreds of dollars' worth of machine tools and parts to adopt this final brilliant design. Leo had Hawaiian and steel guitar sounds in mind, 'subtle vibratos' and glissandi. The Jimi Hendrix innovations of 'divebombing' and detuning were clearly inconceivable in 1954. Again Leo simply opened a window that players leapt through with enthusiasm.

The misnomer 'Tremolo' is Leo's and has virtually reinvented the word for two generations of guitarists. Leo was not a guitarist and he confused the notions of 'vibrato' (a note with a wavering pitch) with 'tremolo' (a rapidly repeated note similar to mandolin technique, or as in Francisco Tarrega's famous study). British guitarists were amongst the first to truly embrace the potential of this device. In the early '60s Hank Marvin invented a whole playing style built on the subtle portamento and vibrato potential of Leo's innovation. Now, in the early 21st century, Jeff Beck has taken the whole thing a stage further, virtually inventing a whole new Stratocaster techniques repertoire. *See page 39*, for more on this important feature.

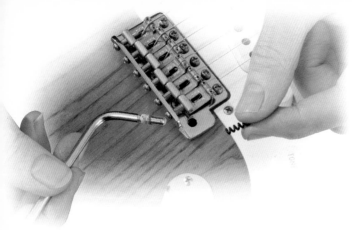

It's worth noting that the tremolo/vibrato arm, or 'whammy bar', is supposed to be held in a suitable playing position by a tiny spring, which creates simple friction pressure on the base of the arm. This spring is often lost, as many players don't even

know it's supposed to be there. It is ⁵⁄₃₂in in diameter and 0.5in long. For replacement, see *Contacts* in the Appendix.

Access to the 'tremolo' mechanism is via a rear plastic panel incorporating string threading holes.

■ Micro Adjustable Bridge

The Stratocaster set a standard with its introduction of a bridge mechanism that allowed individual adjustment of both the height and the length of each string. Ironically the precise clarity of the sound Leo achieved with his single-coil pickups made this innovation a necessity, and like so many innovations it now seems obvious. The Gibson company were tackling the same challenges with their 'tunomatic' solution, but Leo's solution adopts a more blatant 'engineering' approach. This was more acceptable on a revolutionary design like the Strat than on a contemporary Gibson guitar, where a more 'evolutionary' approach was adopted to the development of the electric guitar. For Leo the individual string intonation adjustment was an evolution from work on the significantly titled Precision bass, not the Telecaster guitar, though the Stratocaster was the first to actually feature this solution as standard equipment. The bass finally acquired this facility in 1957 and the Telecaster in 1983!

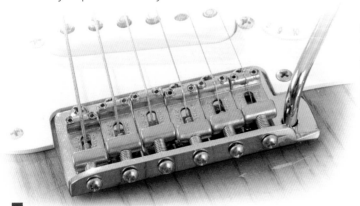

■ Recessed Jacksocket

Yet another innovation – much easier to handle than the edge-fixed socket on the Telecaster and 1951 Precision bass. This meant extensive design work and retooling – not a cheap option.

■ Strap button

You don't really sit down to play a Stratocaster – this guitar was designed for 'Western Swing'.

■ String Guide

A simple design that improves the engagement of the strings at the guitar nut. As page 76 illustrates, this innovation has undergone several redesigns.

■ Three Pickups

These are a refinement on Leo's Telecaster design. The pickups feature 'harmonic positioning'. The neck pickup is positioned at a point to most emphasise the fundamental harmonic, the bridge pickup to most emphasise the higher order harmonics. The middle pickup sits between the two.

■ Enclosed Machine Heads

Not a first but still quite novel. Enclosed machines were in fact known in the 19th century, but they became more of a necessity in the gritty environment of Texas hoe-downs. Leo was wholly practical. He didn't make his own initially but bought them in from the specialist Kluson company. Fender have made their own since 1967 (actually made for them by Schaller but branded as Fender).

■ Single Row Machines

Having the machines on the player's side of the neck in a single accessible row is again not a first but another example of Leo and his team 'pulling together' the world's best design concepts into one whole instrument.

■ Four Bolt Neck

This simple and effective design was briefly compromised during the much-maligned period when CBS owned Fender in the mid-'60s. However, Jimi Hendrix coaxed many a good tune out of CBS Fenders with three-bolt necks.

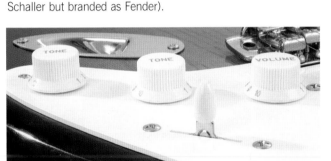

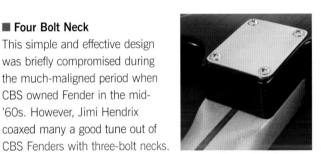

■ Three-Way Pickup Selector Switch

Leo was quite content with this three-position switch and objected to what he called the 'snarl' effect of the combinations of Stratocaster pickups. However, players soon devised the devious use of matchsticks jammed in the socket groove to effect the ear-tingling 'phase' effects thus achieved. Reissue Vintage Fenders come with both three- and five-way switches for ease of use and practical onstage application.

■ Volume and Tone Potentiometers

Resistive capacitor circuits – a simple arrangement familiar to Leo from his days repairing radios. The resistive capacitor circuit de-emphasises selected frequencies in the pickup circuit of the middle and neck pickups.

■ Pickguard

Single-ply plastic or anodised metal pickguard and electronics mount – an innovation which Leo enjoyed, as this meant all the guitar's electrics were assembled as a one-piece single mount component. From c1959 the single-ply was replaced by a triple-ply assembly that was less inclined to warping and cracking. The new fingerboard sometimes incorporated a metal layer intended to improve electronic screening.

The two fingerboards are not interchangeable due to an eight- screw assembly becoming eleven-screw for the laminated version. See page 66 for more on screening issues.

■ 'Spaghetti' Logo

It's not a 'Vintage' Stratocaster without one! Other Stratocasters have modified Fender logos affixed to a range of differing headstocks.

Know your 'American Series'

In 2006 the 'American Series' Strat represents the current standard 'American Stratocaster'. Visually it is very much based on the classic Vintage Strat but with many subtle enhancements and updates to perhaps better adapt the guitar to the realities of gigging in the 21st century.

LEFT The redesigned bridge saddles on an 'American Series' Strat.

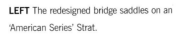

RIGHT A current 'American Series' Strat.

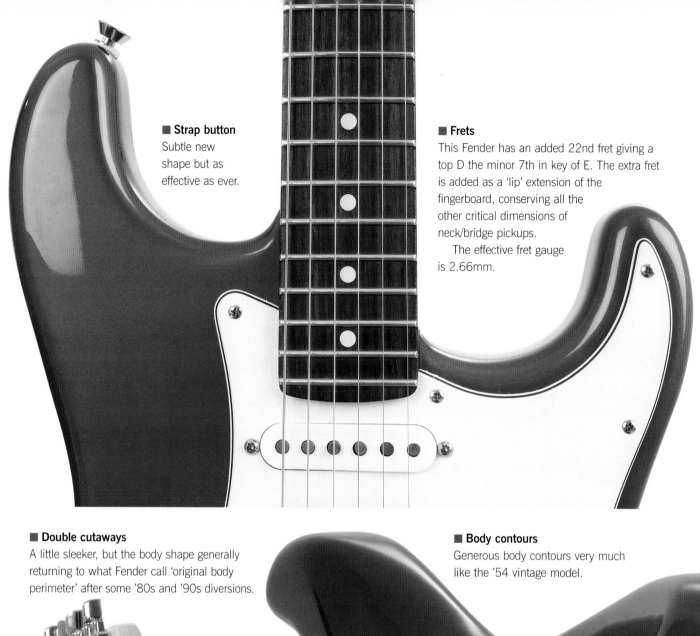

■ **Strap button**
Subtle new shape but as effective as ever.

■ **Frets**
This Fender has an added 22nd fret giving a top D the minor 7th in key of E. The extra fret is added as a 'lip' extension of the fingerboard, conserving all the other critical dimensions of neck/bridge pickups.
The effective fret gauge is 2.66mm.

■ **Double cutaways**
A little sleeker, but the body shape generally returning to what Fender call 'original body perimeter' after some '80s and '90s diversions.

■ **Body contours**
Generous body contours very much like the '54 vintage model.

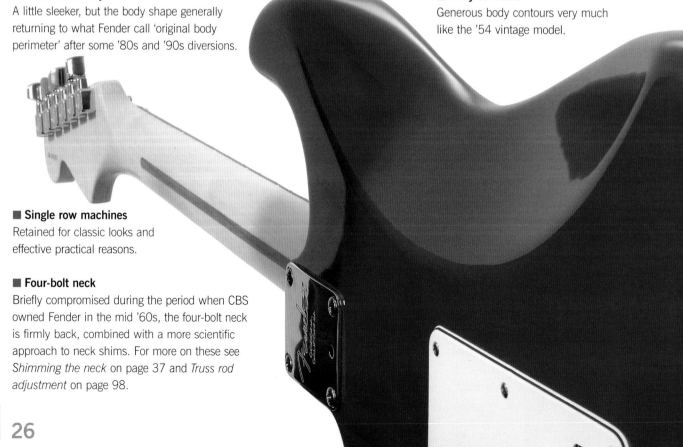

■ **Single row machines**
Retained for classic looks and effective practical reasons.

■ **Four-bolt neck**
Briefly compromised during the period when CBS owned Fender in the mid '60s, the four-bolt neck is firmly back, combined with a more scientific approach to neck shims. For more on these see *Shimming the neck* on page 37 and *Truss rod adjustment* on page 98.

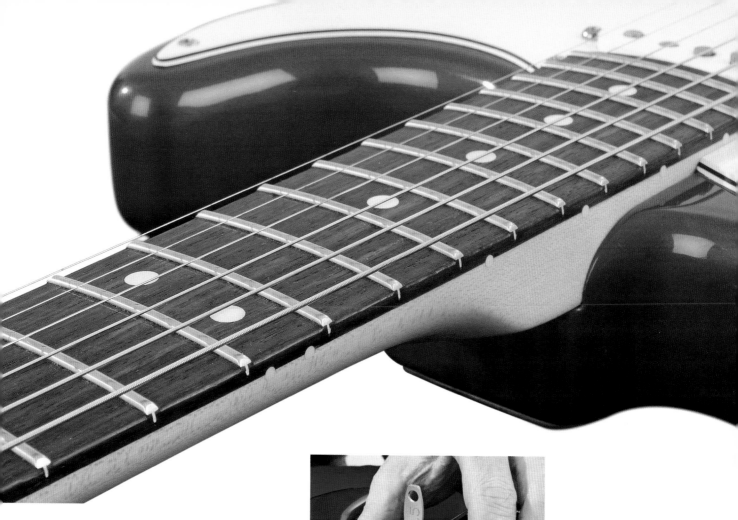

■ Position markers

No change – no flash mother of pearl, just workaday dots – very in keeping with the classic vibe.

■ Maple neck with rosewood fingerboard

This is an adoption of the classic late '50s early '60s approach with a harder rosewood fingerboard still fitted to a softer maple neck.

The fingerboard radius has increased, facilitating string bending without 'choking'. The radius is now 9.5in as opposed to the vintage 7.5in.

The neck edges are subtly rolled for a 'played in' feel. The neck contour is a 'C' style not unlike the early '60s version. See *Neck contours* in the appendix for more on this.

The new neck features a double or 'Bi-flex' truss rod which is a mechanical improvement facilitating more versatile and comprehensive adjustment. The adjustment access has moved, from the inaccessible butt end area to the much more convenient headstock arrangement. This requires a ⅛in Allen key or hex wrench.

■ 'Spaghetti' Logo

Not quite the original, but with a certain retro taste.

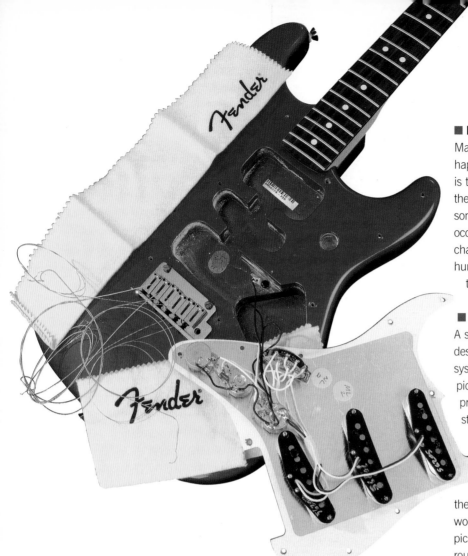

■ Body

Made of alder and not veneered, as sometimes happened in the interim. The biggest difference is that the body is once again only routed for the pickups, not carved out hollow as with some interim strats – this false economy led to occasional warping and a change in sound character. The rout is however pre cut for humbuckers. The finish is polyurethane not the traditional nitrocellulose.

■ Three pickups

A slightly hotter bridge pickup is designed to work with the 'Delta tone' system (see below for more on this). The pickups are also designed with a properly aligned set of pole pieces staggered to accommodate the normal stringing used these days, which includes a plain steel third. Some players will miss the slight eccentricity of the old pole stagger designed for a wound third, the norm in 1954. The pickup covers are sharply edged, not rounded as in the 1954 example.

■ Tremolo/Vibrato access cover

This is now also triple-ply, avoiding the tendency to crack at the screw countersinks observed in the vintage model. Note also the single cavity access as opposed to the original six-hole type.

■ Tremolo/Vibrato

This version is only slightly 'improved' from Leo's original concept. The significant difference is the more precise two-point fulcrum.

■ Micro adjustable bridge

The micro adjustable bridge benefits these days from compressed stainless steel saddles. These have more mass than the vintage pressed steel types. They are less prone to corrosion and have a slightly different sound quality. In theory they should produce a little more sustain as well as being more stable.

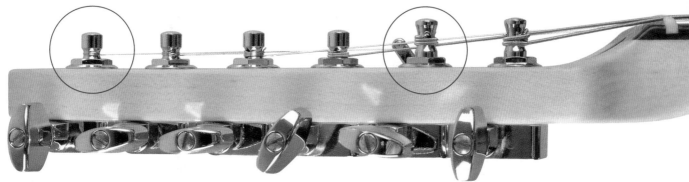

■ Enclosed machine heads

The current Strat has custom-made Schallers, good machine heads with better mechanics than the old Klusons. As highlighted above, this custom variant cleverly staggers the string posts to give a good downward pressure at the nut on all strings.

■ Pickguard

From c1959 the single-ply was replaced by a triple-ply assembly that was less inclined to warping and cracking. The new fingerboard sometimes incorporated a metal layer intended to improve electronic screening. The vintage fingerboards are not interchangeable due to an eight-screw assembly becoming eleven-screw for the laminated version. See *Screening and RF induction* on page 66 for more on screening issues.

The American series has a subtle parchment-white colouring to the plastic for a slightly vintage vibe.

■ Volume and tone potentiometers

Still very simple but effective, the new Strat incorporates 'Delta tone' pots which provide no resistive load and consequently a subtly different tone contour.

■ Five-way pickup selector switch

Whatever Leo might have personally thought the five-way switch is here to stay. Most current Strats incorporate phase cancellation wiring in the 'combined' pickup positions, giving a pseudo humbucking effect.

■ Recessed jacksocket

An almost permanent Strat feature, it did go missing briefly as a CBS false economy but is now standard again.

■ String guide

The sexy new double guide is designed for minimum resistance to string movement when tuning, or when using the vibrato. Together with the clever staggering of the string posts on the new machine heads a good angle is achieved to create enough pressure at the nut.

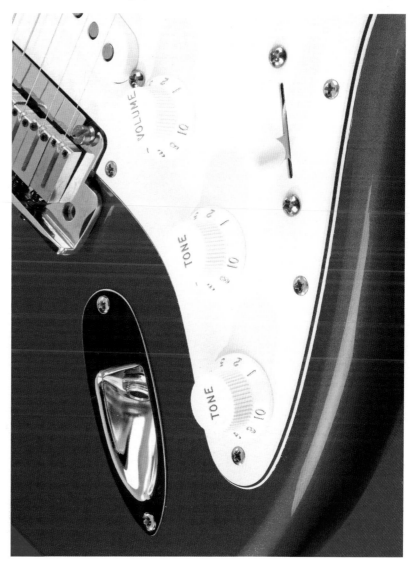

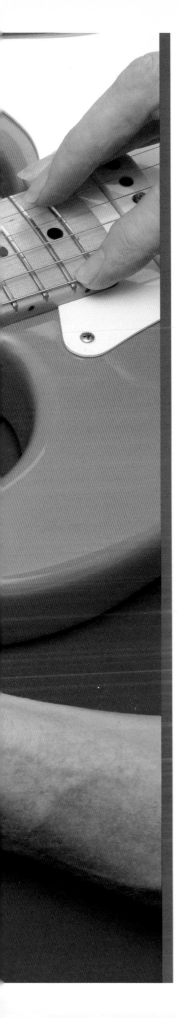

Setting up and tuning

Achieving the perfect 'action' for your style of playing. A properly set up budget 'Squier' is a far more useful guitar than a poorly aligned Custom Shop Limited Edition. It is almost impossible to tune a poorly set up guitar.

LEFT Checking the neck relief on a '57 Fiesta Red.

RIGHT Note the wear on this maple fingerboard.

Setting the string heights

One of the joys of Leo Fender's original no-nonsense design is the ability (for the first time ever in a production instrument) to adjust individual string heights as well as effective string length.

■ Action

It is extremely important to note that a guitar's 'string action' is affected by a complex interplay of factors, not just the bridge height setting.

Factors to consider:

■ The nut height setting and individual nut grooves.
■ Neck relief – is the neck flat, convex or, ideally, slightly concave along its length? (when strung)
■ Fret wear – are the frets correctly 'stoned' or is wear causing these to be uneven?
■ Is the fingerboard radius reflected in the individual bridge saddle alignment?
■ Does the neck/body angle as determined by 'shims', or Micro-Tilt adjustment in later post-Vintage Strats, need attention?
■ Are the string gauges appropriate and 'matched' as a set?

All of these issues are addressed below.

⚡ Tech Tip

If you can't achieve a workable action with the bridge grub screws set at their lowest then you probably need a shim in the neck cavity.

John Diggins – Luthier

■ So why might you want to adjust individual string height?

The most likely reason is to correctly reflect the radius of the fingerboard, or perhaps you're just curious. Leo would approve – he built his whole Fender guitar concept around satisfying individual player's requirements. This built-in versatility has resulted in one genius design being used happily by players as diverse as Hank Marvin, Jimi Hendrix, and Joe Walsh. More likely you're trying to achieve a lower, more playable action.

Perhaps you're experimenting with string gauges? Following a change of string gauges – particularly moving up to a heavier gauge for a Stevie Ray Vaughan sound or even an early Hank Marvin sound – you may find the neck has become more

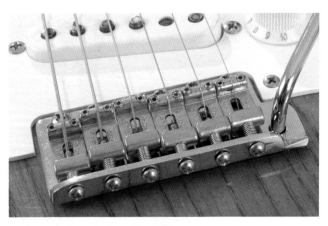

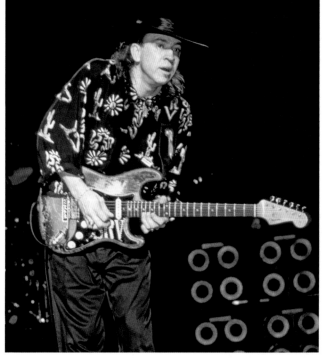

Innovation

As a working engineer Leo would have been aware that the Gretsch company had introduced individual string length adjustment in 1952 with the six-saddle Melita Synchro-sonic bridge, designed by Sebastiano (Johnny) Melita, and Gibson had introduced their 'Tunomatic' bridge c1953.

For details of your specific Stratocaster neck radius see the case studies in this book or use a radius gauge.

■ Another important factor

Before adjusting the saddles it is also worth checking the nut. A good guide for correct Stratocaster nut height for conventional playing (ie non-slide playing) is approximately .008in–.010in at the first fret. Check this by inserting a car feeler gauge (.010in) at the first fret: it should be a close fit but not lifting the string.

If the nut is too high or too low, either generally or on one particular string, then refer to 'Nut adjustment' page 90.

concave along its length – 'done a Robin Hood' is one affectionate technical term for this. The neck has perhaps bowed.

You may first need to adjust the truss rod to compensate for this. If you suspect this is the case see 'Truss rod adjustment' page 98 for Fender 'neck relief' specifications and remedies. Having adjusted the truss rod it's likely you may also want to reset the string action for optimum comfort appropriate to your own style of playing.

If you're playing bottleneck guitar you may need to set the strings quite high to avoid catching the frets with your slide.

If you're playing slinky blues with a light picking style you may find a very 'low' action workable.

String height parameters eventually come down to personal taste and your individual sound. However, Leo did offer some recommendations for 'average' set-ups:

Neck radius	String height Bass side	String height Treble side
7.25in	⁴⁵⁄₆₄in/.7081in	⁴⁄₆₄in/¹⁄₁₆in/.0625in
9.5in to 12in	⁴⁄₆₄in	⁴⁄₆₄in
15in to 17in	⁴⁄₆₄in	³⁄₆₄in/.0469in

1 Check the current action height at the 17th fret with the car feeler gauge. In practice this means either combining several individual feeler gauges to make up ⅟₁₆in or the decimal equivalent value of .0625in, or, using a 6in ruler (with ⅟₃₂in and ⅟₆₄in increments), measuring the distance between the bottom of the strings and the top of the 17th fret.

2 With a .050in Allen key, use the two pivot adjustment screws to achieve the desired overall string height for the first string at the 17th fret. Vintage guide height is ⁴⁄₆₄in (⅟₁₆in/.0625in) on the classic 7.25in radius.

✎ Tech Tip

I find it best to set the first string height first. Set the first string high enough to avoid 'choking' when bending the string in the high fret positions. The other string heights should follow the neck radius pattern.

John Diggins – Luthier

✎ Tech Tip

Should you lose one of the screws the threads on the Vintage saddles tiny grub screws are 4-40 UNC.

John Diggins – Luthier

■ Adjust the sixth string bridge saddle to the 'Vintage' ⁵⁄₆₄in height according to the Fender chart recommendations, then adjust the other bridge saddles to follow the neck radius as indicated by the appropriate under-string radius gauge. NB: For proprietary radius gauges please see *Contacts* in the appendix.

■ **Re-tune the guitar**

These recommended action settings and radius measurements are, of course, only a guide. You can obviously experiment with the individual saddle height until your desired sound and feel is achieved.

Note that adjusting string heights affects the effective sounding length of the string, and this naturally affects intonation, so you may now need to refer to Part 2 of this chapter, 'Setting the working string length'.

It is important to note that the magnetic field of the conventional Strat pickup can be strong enough to interfere with the string's normal excursion, and this can have further implications for accurate intonation – see *Setting pickup heights* on page 84 for more on this.

2 Bridge adjustment

Setting the working string length

Leo Fender's original design incorporated the ability to adjust individual string lengths.

■ So why would you want to do this?

If the guitar has not been maintained for some years, or if you have recently changed your string gauges, you may notice that as you ascend the fingerboard in normal playing the guitar is not sounding 'in tune'.

■ A little background information

There are two basic ways of changing the pitch of a vibrating guitar string – you can increase or decrease the string tension by adjusting the machine heads, as in normal tuning, or you can alter the string length by normal fretting on the fingerboard.

The frets on the fingerboard are arranged in a mathematical series of ascending decreasing intervals. The frets get closer together as we ascend to 'the dusty end of the fingerboard'. We won't get bogged down in the maths here, but you could perhaps impress the drummer by dropping the phrases 'rule of 18' or 'Pythagorean equation' into the pre-gig drinks conversation. Look it up it may inspire a new song.

The assumption of the correct function of the carefully worked out fret intervals is that the string itself has a defined length. If all your guitar's strings were the same gauge or thickness we could dispense with Leo's invention and simply have a 'straight line' arrangement of the bridge saddles.

In the real world your first string could be .009 gauge and your sixth string .042. The other four strings are usually gauged somewhere between these two. Fretting a string changes its tension slightly. A difference in string diameter affects the amount of change in string tension as it is fretted. This means that to sound 'in tune' the first string benefits from having a shorter effective length than the second string and so on. Hence Leo's innovation.

Find a gauge of string that works for you, set the guitar up and stick with that gauge.

NB: The chrome bridge cover if present should be removed. Though they are part of Leo Fender's original concept, bridge covers are rarely found on Strats in practical use, as they prevent the use of right-hand damping or 'etouffe' effects. Guitarists affectionately refer to these redundant parts as Fender 'ashtrays'.

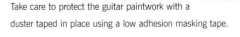

Take care to protect the guitar paintwork with a duster taped in place using a low adhesion masking tape.

1 Tune the open string to E concert. Check the harmonic note at the 12th fret of the first string as compared to the same fretted note (no pun intended, but clearly the harmonic note contains less of the 'fundamental' pitch note than the fretted note; this should not affect the adjustment). All the sounded notes should be precisely the same pitch though in different octaves. A practised ear will detect any discrepancy. An alternative solution is to use an extremely accurate electronic tuner, which will visually display any discrepancy in 'cents', either 'flat' or 'sharp'.

Tools required

- Phillips-type screwdriver size '0' or'1'
- Electronic tuner (optional) Guitar lead
- Duster and masking tape

2 If the string sounds or indicates 'flat' at the 12th fret when compared with the 12th harmonic, turn the longitudinal screw anti-clockwise, thereby moving the saddle towards the neck.

If the note at the 12th fret sounds 'sharp' as compared to the harmonic then the string length is too short and the saddle should be adjusted clockwise.

Adjust until the harmonic, open string, and 12th fret all indicate or sound at the same pitch. Repeat this procedure for all six strings.

Note that raising or lowering the string saddles as in Part 1 of this chapter, 'Setting the string height', will effectively alter the string length so essentially these two operations should be considered together.

🔧 Tech Tip

It's worth checking the intonation at the 19th fret of the first string (B natural) against the open B string. If the open B and E are in tune then the 19th fret and open B should not 'beat'. This applies equally to the 20th fret on the B string and the open G string. Similar checks should be tried on the 19th fret for all the other strings.

John Diggins – Luthier

Neck adjustment

Shimming the neck on a Vintage Strat

Another important factor to consider with Strat neck adjustment is the precise 'pitch' of the neck in relation to the body (this implies changing the angle of the neck slightly in the neck socket, thereby 'pitching' the neck away from the body). A wooden 'shim' .010in (0.25mm) thick is placed in the neck pocket, underneath the end of the neck.

A new shim approximately .5in (12.8mm) wide x 1.75in (44.5mm) long x .010in (0.25mm) thick will allow you to raise the action approximately ½in (0.8mm).

■ So why would you want to do this?

The need to adjust the pitch of the neck occurs in situations where the string height is high and the action adjustment is as low as the adjustment will allow.

'Shimming' is the time-honoured procedure used to adjust the pitch of the Vintage Strat neck. The pitch of the neck on your guitar should have been preset at the factory and in most cases will not need to be adjusted. However, old Strats have often been repaired/adjusted and 'shims' are often lost or removed accidentally.

⚡ Tech Tip

Shims can be made of card or bits of old-fashioned electrical insulating board. I prefer thin wood veneers: this seems organic – wood to wood contact.

John Diggins – Luthier

1 Slacken the strings and partly unscrew the four neck screws using a size '2' point Phillips screwdriver. Always mask the paintwork on a valuable instrument (illustrated is a Chinese Squier). Slacken the 'back' screws more extensively as illustrated.

2 Ease the neck gently from its seating in the pocket of the body.

3 Place the new shim in position and carefully hold its position by replacing the neck in its slot and retightening the neck fixing screws.

4 Adjust the string height and bridge radius as per this chapter. As with most modern Strats, the fingerboard radius of this Chinese-made model is 9.5in.

⚡ Tech Tip

If you can't achieve a workable action with the grub screws set at their lowest then you probably need a shim in the neck cavity. Also, a good rough guide for action setting is to put the .50in Allen key under the 21st fret. If it fits, the action is in the right area.

John Diggins – Luthier

Replacing Kluson tuners

Early and valuable Strats are usually fitted with Kluson Deluxe semi-enclosed machine heads. These were the most easily available at the time of manufacture but are not perfect. They have a tendency to a 'dead spot', which means turning the tuner in opposite directions often has no effect on the string post and therefore the string tension. The 'dead spot' is caused by poor manufacturing tolerances and the use of brass for the worm gear as opposed to steel.

Fortunately Spertzel and Gotoh now manufacture an exact lookalike with the advantage of a better gearing ratio – 15:1 rather than the old 12:1 – and with nylon washers to take up any slack in the worm gear.

■ Simply remove the strings following the usual procedures and place the lookalike tuners in the existing slots using a Phillips '0' point or '1' point screwdriver depending on the guitar in question.

■ Remember to replace the ferrules.

■ Occasionally there may be some slight difference in the size of the 'bushings' on replacements. The correct solution is to file the serrated teeth on the new bushings rather than deface a vintage guitar.

Keep old parts

When replacing any parts on a vintage guitar to preserve the guitar's looks and value, get the nearest you can to an identical replacement and store all the vintage parts safely. They will help provide provenance for the instrument at any future sale.

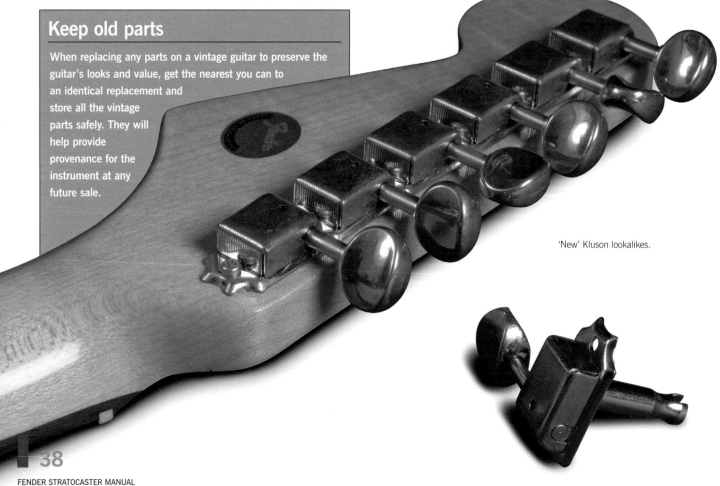

'New' Kluson lookalikes.

Tremolo/Vibrato alignment

This alignment applies to the vintage-style 'synchronised' tremolo.

There are also other Strat and retro-fit trems available these days. For information on these see *Specific Case Studies* particularly the *American Series* on page 140 and the *Mexican-made Fat Strat* on page 118.

■ Before beginning alignment – Check the 'bevel'

Leo designed his tremolo on a very simple 'knife-edge' principle, which he first observed working effectively on a set of kitchen 'balance' weighing scales. This was exactly the principle he required, and depended on the strings providing one weight on the 'balance' and his tremolo springs the other. To work correctly this relies on a knife-edge between the bridge fixing screws and a countersunk hole in the bottom of the bridge plate.

It is worth checking for the correct bevel on the pivot points underneath the bridge. These could be worn or, more rarely, have never been quite right since manufacture.

1 Remove the guitar strings – I recommend doing this one at a time and working from the sixth and first inwards towards the fourth and third. This method prevents damage and misalignment caused by too much sudden stress and change in the neck tension.

2 Using a '1' point Phillips screwdriver, carefully remove the plastic access cover located on the back of the guitar. Use a small plastic tray or paint-can lid to store the temporarily removed screws.

3 Unclip the tremolo springs – this may require a small set of pliers.

4 Unscrew the six bridge retaining screws with a '2' point Phillips screwdriver.

5 Examine the under bridge countersink. The rim should be between ³⁄₆₄in and ¹⁄₁₆in thick and should be consistent for all six screws. If you decide to adjust the bevel you'll require a 'No 4' metalworkers' countersink. Do not contemplate this unless you're a skilled metalworker, as precision is required.

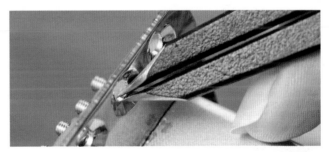

6 Apply a small amount of Vaseline or similar at the pivot contact points of the bridge to ensure smooth and accurate operation.

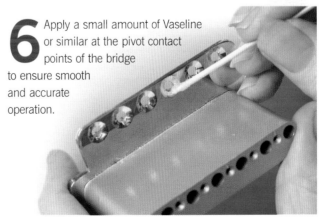

■ Reassembling the bridge

When replacing the bridge retaining screws follow the instructions given in Steps 3 and 4 below. The tremolo springs must be back in place in order to set the bridge screw heights.

Restring the guitar but leave the tremolo rear access plate off for now.

■ Alignment Procedure

The Fender 'floating tremolo' design relies on establishing a balance between a consistent string tension and the set tension of the vibrato spring mechanism. If this balance is incorrect the vibrato will not function correctly; it will also be difficult to string the guitar via the rear access holes, as they're likely to be misaligned. In fact many Vintage Strats are missing the rear vibrato cover due to frustration over this issue.

■ START HERE
If aligning the trem without checking the bevel

1 Using a '1' point Phillips screwdriver carefully remove the plastic access cover located on the back of the guitar. Use a small plastic lid or Fender ashtray to store the screws.

As so often happens Eric Clapton has permenantly removed the rear access plate on 'Blackie'. Note also the blocked off trem and five springs.

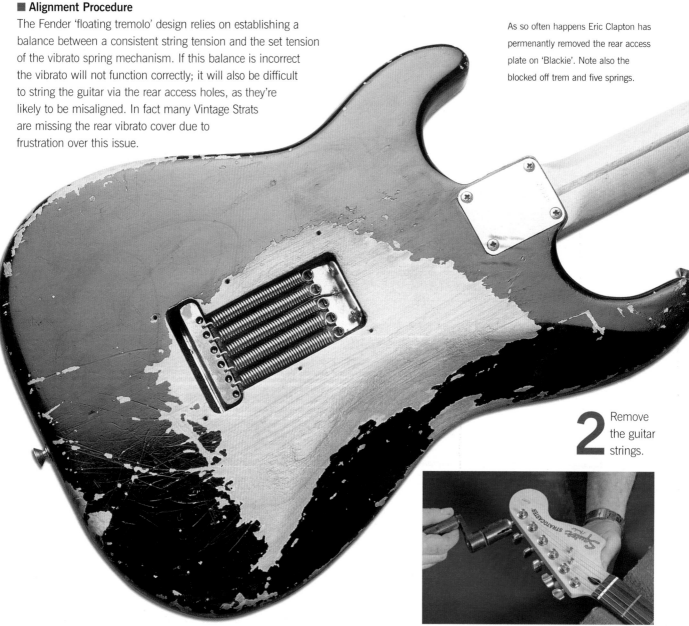

2 Remove the guitar strings.

3 Using a '1' point Phillips screwdriver loosen all six screws located at the front edge of the bridge plate. Raise them so that all of the screws measure approximately 1/16in (1.6mm) above the top of the bridge plate.

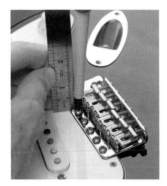

4 Now tighten the two outside screws until they're flush with the top of the bridge plate. Then loosen these two screws a quarter-turn. The bridge will pivot on the outside screws, leaving the four inside screws in place for bridge stability.

5 Restring the guitar and check your guitar is at either (a) standard pitch or (b) a custom pitch that you're opting to use consistently with this particular guitar. Use an electronic tuner set to your favoured pitch.

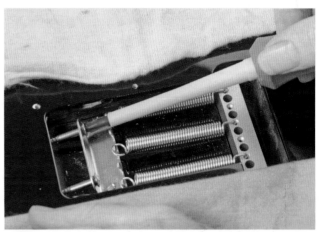

6 Ensuring that the bridge can float freely (no obstruction of the tremolo arm), use a '2' point Phillips screwdriver to adjust the 'claw' screws in the tremolo cavity.

■ Adjust the bridge to your desired angle (Fender factory specification is a 1/8in/3.2mm gap at the rear of the bridge, which is a good starting point).

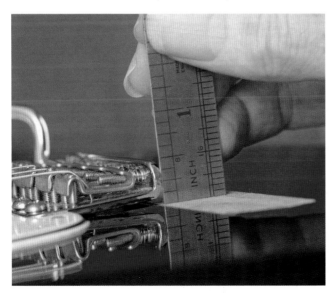

7 **Note** that you'll need to retune as required to get the right balance between the strings and the springs.

■ If you prefer a flush bridge to the body, adjust the spring tension to equal the string tension whilst the bridge rests on the body (you may want to add an extra half-turn to each claw screw to ensure that the bridge remains flush to the body during string bends).

CAUTION: Do not over-tighten these springs, as this can put unnecessary tension on the arm during tremolo use.

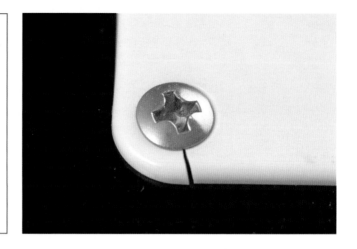

Tech Tip

Generally if the pivot is correctly engineered – and sometimes it does require a little subtle re-filing and sometimes 'centring' – then no lubrication is necessary. If you're having severe tuning problems take the guitar to an expert.

John Diggins – Luthier

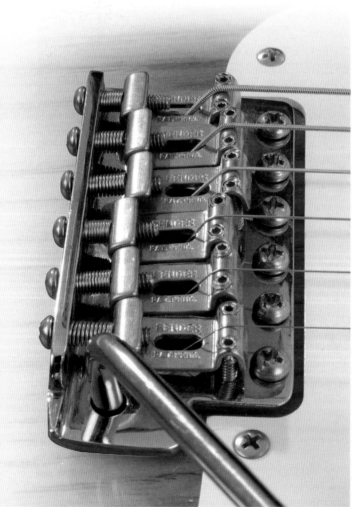

8 Once your Strat is aligned it is essential to maintain a consistent use of string type, gauge, and even manufacture, as tensions will otherwise vary, causing imbalances and tuning instability.

9 Replace rear cover using type '1' Phillips as before. Take care not to over-tighten the screws, as the thin plastic will tend to crack at the edges.

Tech Tip

The vintage Strat has a tiny (22 gauge, approximately ⁵⁄₃₂in) spring in the tremolo arm screw cavity. This is designed to keep the arm under tension and in a suitable playing position. This works well in the original Leo Fender steel-made cavity. On later cast alloy versions it can often strip the tremolo arm thread and may be better disposed of. A little Loctite left to set on the thread will usually provide enough torque to keep the trem/vibrato arm in position.

John Diggins – Luthier

A properly set up Stratocaster will tune up and stay in tune better than any electric solid body guitar (except Leo's own Telecaster family) had ever done before 1954. What makes this even more remarkable is the potential instability of the synchronised tremolo.

When the Stratocaster first appeared the only reference options available for accurate tuning were tuning forks as used by violinists and piano tuners, and 'pitch pipes', a device similar to a mouth organ with six 'open string' reference pitches. Pianos were often pitched fractionally flat due to neglect.

Additionally, there was some consternation over the Strats perceived need to be at concert pitch A-440 in order to function correctly. In the '50s and '60s many guitar bands often tuned at arbitrary pitch. Absolute pitch only became an issue when keyboards or wind instruments became part of the band's line-up. In fact, as you now know, the Stratocaster tremolo springs can be easily adjusted (see this chapter) to cope with a range of guitar pitches.

The introduction of electronic tuners since the early '80s has offered guitarists an increasingly accurate reference tool. The key word here is 'reference'. The open strings of a guitar tuned to correspond with an accurate electronic tuner provide a great starting point for accurate tuning. However, it's essential to remember that the guitar, like the piano, is a tempered instrument. Even the most accurately fretted and set up Stratocaster is built on a tempered tuning system that compromises the science of pitch by considering 'enharmonic' notes such as C# and Db as the same note, which they are not!

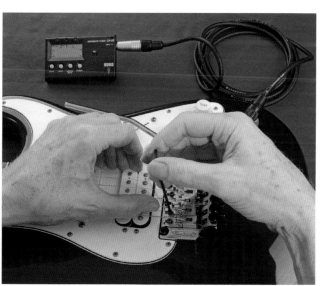

Under the recording microscope

In the 1970s and 1980s I worked as an engineer and producer for BBC Radio One. In that role I encountered many young bands during their first serious recording sessions. Most had never had their guitars set up properly and virtually all were unaware of the wider scope of guitar tuning beyond tuning the open strings via an electronic tuner. Consequently, many a frustrating hour of valuable session time was spent adjusting string lengths and tempering guitar tunings to the key of the song to be recorded. Always check your set-up before an important recording session.

■ Tempered Tuning

If we all played fretless guitars this would not be an issue. However, there are very few fretless Stratocasters and even less fretless guitarists.

■ Tempered Tuning in Practice

In the real world a tuning compromise has been reached, referred to as 'equal temperament', and most rock and pop musicians will happily accept the faint 'out of tuneness' associated with certain chords in certain keys and positions on the fingerboard.

In fact in single string solo playing many players consciously or unconsciously temper certain notes slightly sharp or flat by a combination of listening and microtonally bending notes as they play. This technique combined with pitch-dependent vibrato is so indigenous to the guitar as to be second nature. This factor even contributes to the guitars expressive 'human' quality – keyboards, for instance, can never really do this.

For accurate rhythm playing which naturally incorporates chords many guitarists will tune to key, using an electronic tuner for reference and then tempering the relevant notes within the pivotal chords of a song to reach an acceptable compromise that sounds musical.

■ The Bottom Line

Tune your Strat to EADGBE (or whatever exotic tuning you favour) using a tuner for reference, then temper as required.

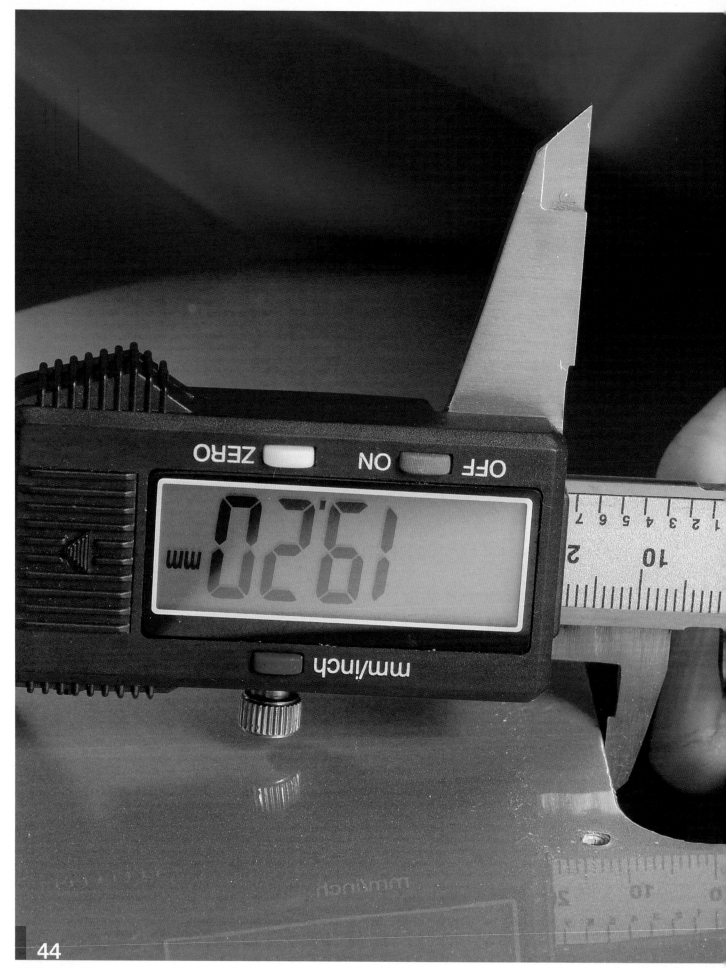

Repairs, maintenance and adjustments

An electric guitar is a mechanical device subject to wear and tear. As such it obviously benefits from a little maintenance and lubrication. Some tasks are open to player attention but beware of skilled areas such as paintwork retouching unless you have the tools and experience.

LEFT Measuring up for 'blocked off' trem.

RIGHT An American Deluxe.

Safety first

Generally speaking the electric guitar is no more dangerous to play or to work on than its acoustic cousin. However, there are inevitably some additional hazards of which you should be aware.

Electric shock

Sadly many guitar players have either been killed or badly burned through accidental exposure to mains current. Though the UK's adoption of 240V may seem to present a greater risk than the USA's 110V, it's actually the amps that are the killer, not the volts! Amperes are the measure of current, and high currents are the ones to avoid.

Guitar amplifiers run happily on domestic supplies at relatively low current ratings, so the situation of one guitarist one amp is a pretty safe scenario, especially if we observe a few precautions:

■ Always ensure a good earth or ground connection. This allows a safe path to earth for any stray current, which always flows along the easiest path. The earth or ground connection offers a quicker route to earth than through you and therein lies its safety potential.

■ Never replace fuses with others of the wrong value, eg a 5-amp fuse in a 3-amp socket. Fuses are there to protect us and our equipment from power surges. A higher value means less protection. Never replace a fuse with a bodge such as silver foil or similar. This offers no protection at all.

■ Consider using an earth leakage trip or similar circuit-breaker in any situation where you have no control over or knowledge of the mains power.

■ Maintain your mains leads. Check them regularly for damage and strained wires.

■ Never operate an amplifier with the safety cover removed, especially valve amplifiers known for their HT circuits.

■ Never put drinks on or near amplifiers.

■ Never touch a lighting circuit or lamp. Apart from mains electricity issues they are often also dangerously hot. Leave lamps to qualified electricians.

Beware of

■ Multi amp/multi PA scenarios that aren't professionally administered. Professional PA and lighting supervisors are very safety-conscious these days and are trained in health and safety to a legal minimum requirement. The danger comes with 'semi pro' and amateur rigs which aren't closely scrutinised. If you're in any doubt don't plug in until you've talked to the on site supervisor and feel you can trust his assurances.

■ Unknown stage situations, especially those which feature big lighting rigs. This is easily said but hard to adhere to. Even the most modest gigs nowadays have quite sophisticated lights and sound. The crucial issue is that all the audio equipment is connected to the same PHASE. Danger particularly arises when microphones are connected to one PHASE and guitars to another. A guitar/vocalist could find himself as the 'bridge' between 30 amps of current! If in any doubt be rude and ask.

Hearing damage

Leo Fender's first guitar amp, the K&F of 1945, knocked out a feverish 4W of audio. In fact they were so mild mannered that some of them lacked so much as a volume control.

The first Fender Bassman amps boasted 26W and by 1964 The Beatles had the first 100W VOX amps, specifically made to cope with concerts in vast football stadiums and the noise of immense screaming crowds.

By 1970 100W was the norm for a guitar 'head' in a small club and the first 10,000W PA systems had rocked Woodstock.

Pete Townshend of The Who first complained of the hearing impairment tinnitus in the mid '70s and for many years refused to tour with a band as his hearing worsened. The key to saving your hearing is 'dose' figures. Research has shown that you risk damage if exposed to sound 'dose' levels of 90dB or above for extended periods. Health and safety limits for recording studios now recommend no more than 90dBA ('A' standing for average) per eight-hour day, these levels to be reduced dramatically if the period is longer or the dBA higher.

Transient peaks, as in those produced by a loud snare drum or hi-hat, can easily push levels beyond these figures. Be careful where you stand in relation to drums and amplifiers – a small movement can effect a dramatic change in transient sound level. Don't be afraid to ask about peak and average levels. Your ears are your greatest asset as a musician, so don't be embarrassed into thinking you can't question sound levels.

Repetitive strain injury
Guitarists need to think about posture, warm-up routines, and avoiding over-practising. RSI is not funny and affects millions of guitarists. Generate good habits early and stick to them.

Paints and solvents

Traditionally the Vintage Stratocaster was painted with nitrocellulose lacquer and this practice continues on limited numbers of Vintage Reissues. Nitrocellulose lacquers produce a very hard yet flexible, durable finish that can be polished to a high gloss. The drawbacks of these lacquers include the hazardous nature of the solvent, which is flammable, volatile, and toxic. The dangers inherent in the inhalation of spray paints are serious enough to be covered by legal statutes in the USA, the UK, and Europe.

Symptoms
Acute and chronic ingestion: Large doses may cause nausea, narcosis, weakness, drowsiness, and unconsciousness.

■ Inhalation: Irritation to nose and throat. At high concentrations, same effects as ingestion.
■ Skin: Cracking of skin, dermatitis, and secondary infections.
■ Eyes: Irritation.
■ Symptoms of overexposure: Repeated skin contact may cause dermatitis, while the skin defatting properties of this material may aggravate existing dermatitis.
(Source: Material Safety Data Sheet.)

Polyurethane hazards
Later Stratocasters are almost exclusively painted with polyurethane.

Vapours may accumulate in inadequately ventilated/confined areas. Vapours may form explosive mixtures with air. Vapours may travel long distances and flashback may occur. Closed containers may explode when exposed to extreme heat.

Symptoms
Ingestion: May be similar to inhalation symptoms – drowsiness, dizziness, nausea, irritation of digestive tract, depression, aspiration hazard.

■ Inhalation: Dizziness, drowsiness, fatigue, weakness, headache, unconsciousness.
■ Skin: Drying, cracking, dermatitis.
■ Eyes: Burning, tearing, reddening. Possible transient corneal injury or swelling of conjunctiva.
(Source: Carbon Black Carcinogen by IARC, Symptoms of Overexposure.)

Recommended precautions
Always wear goggles/full face shield and other protective equipment. Avoid skin contact by wearing protective clothing. Take a shower and bathe your eyes after exposure. Wash contaminated clothing thoroughly before reusing it.

...So, with all this in mind, remember that the addresses of recommended guitar repair men and spray shops can be found in your local *Yellow Pages*.

If you really feel you want to customise your Stratocaster's body then you must take extreme precautions, particularly to avoid inhalation of the dangerous mist created by the spray process.

A passive mask available from DIY stores will only offer the most minimal protection. If in any doubt consult the paint manufacturer for detailed precautions specific to the paint type you've chosen.

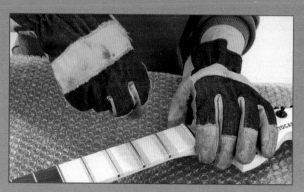

Tools and working facilities

It's worth noting that Leo designed his guitar for adjustment by means of everyday hardware store tools rather than specialist luthiers' equipment. He was clearly inventing the working man's guitar.

Necessary workshop tools

Many of the tools listed below can double up as your essential gig bag wrap, but as you don't have to carry all of them around we can be less concerned about weight and portability. Consequently it's very convenient, for instance, to have separate screwdrivers rather than the interchangeable-bit variety. Heftier wire cutters also make string changing a little easier.

■ Set of car feeler gauges (.002–.025) (0.05–1mm)
These are used for assessing and setting the string action height.

■ Light machine oil (3-in-1 or equivalent)
Can be used sparingly for lubricating the string path.

■ Set of Phillips-type screwdrivers, sizes '0', '1', and '2' point
It may seem a small point but I recommend using the correct size and type of screwdriver. Many valuable Strats that have survived 30 years on the road often have a selection of odd screws and 'stripped' screw heads. These look unsightly, slow down maintenance, and make the simplest job a chore. The correct 'point' screwdriver size will reduce screw stripping and is also less likely to skate across your prized paintwork. The exceptions, of course, are Rory Gallagher or Post Monterey Hendrix/Zappa 'distressed' models.

Use type '0' point for some bridge saddle length adjustments and string guides; type '1' point for pickguard, trem rear cover, jack socket, bridge pivot, machine head (Kluson type), and strap buttons; and type '2' point for pickup height adjustment, neck retaining screws, tremolo springs, trem/block join, and three-pole switch retainers.

A screwdriver with interchangeable heads is an alternative option. However, you'll often need to use several heads at the same time, which means a lot of changing around. This option is nevertheless useful on the road, when a compact toolkit is more practical.

■ A large 1½in straight-blade screwdriver
For Vintage-type truss rods – though many techs use a '2' point Phillips for this.

■ Electronic tuner
An accurate electronic tuner with a jack socket as opposed to an internal microphone will make short work of adjusting the intonation of individual string lengths.

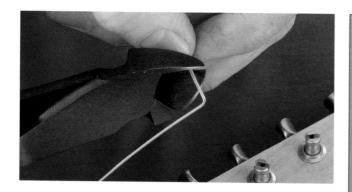

■ Wire cutters

For cutting strings to length. Particularly useful when dealing with Vintage-type machine heads.

■ Peg winder

Time saving, and avoids repetitive strain injury when changing strings.

■ Polish and cloth

A soft duster for the body and the back of the neck, and a lint-free cotton cloth for strings and fingerboard. Proprietary guitar polishes differ from household furniture polishes, which often contain silicone. The wax used in guitar polish is emulsified to avoid any sticky residue, especially under the heat generated by stage lighting.

■ Tweezers

For rescuing dropped screws from awkward cavities and removing hot wires and debris during soldering. Some Vintage Strats still retain cloth wire insulation, which doesn't melt but may start to disintegrate – I don't think anybody expected electric guitars to last 50 years!

■ A small penlight torch

Useful for the closer examination of details at any time, but especially in a stage-side emergency.

■ Allen keys

0.050in size for bridge saddle height adjustment on Vintage and Vintage-type Strats; also correct for the Japanese 'Standard' ⅛in size for truss rod adjustment on late '70s 'bullet' type, and ³⁄₁₆in size for the Mexican 'Standard'. ³⁄₃₂in size for Micro-Tilt neck adjustment on late '70s Strats, and ⅛in size for the current four-bolt neck.

I've detailed more precise Allen key requirements in the individual case study descriptions.

Henry Phillips

Have you ever wondered why Leo went for Phillips-type screws, especially as the Broadcaster had started out equipped with conventional slotted screws? It certainly intrigued me in 1965, as I tried to rescue my 1962 Fiesta Red. As related elsewhere in these pages, this had been stored in a damp loft and the metal parts were very rusty. In 1960s Liverpool it was hard to find a Phillips screwdriver, and impossible to find six different sizes of chrome Phillips screws. I consequently replaced all of them with slotted chrome screws. (If you have my '62 Fiesta Red, serial no 87827, I'd be pleased to hear from you – and, er, sorry about the straight screws.)

In 1953 Leo was very keen on a streamlined assembly process like Henry Ford's car plant in Detroit, and Henry Phillips (1890–1958) had specifically developed his cross-head screw for use in car production lines: in 1936 'The American Screw Co' persuaded General Motors to use the Phillips screw in the manufacture of Cadillacs, and by 1940 virtually every American automaker had switched to Phillips screws.

This new screw worked well with ratchet and electric screwdrivers, had greater torque, was self-centring, and didn't slip from the slot so easily, avoiding damage to the valuable paintjob. The speed with which Phillips screws can be used was crucial to the auto assembly line. In addition, Phillips screws are almost impossible to over-screw, which was very important.

As Leo's fledgling cottage industry started to turn into an assembly line, this was just what he was looking for. In the Stratocaster's first year (1954–5) he made around 700 Strats and as many Telecasters, as well as several hundred basses.

However, cam-out or torque-out makes tightly-driven Phillips screws fiendishly hard to remove and often damages the screw, the driver, and anything else a suddenly loose driver happens to hit. And whereas a coin or a piece of scrap metal can often be used to loosen a slotted screw, nothing can do the job of a Phillips screwdriver. A flat-bladed driver or even a wrong-size Phillips just makes cam-out worse.

Beware: Phillips screwdrivers should not be used with Pozidrive screws (and vice versa). They are subtly different, and when mixed they tend to ride out of the slot as well as rounding the corners of both the tool and the screw recess.

■ Soldering iron

This should be at least 25W
with a penlight tip. An iron is
essential when replacing
worn-out volume pots and
three-way switches, etc. It's
worth investing in a stand
with a sponge cleaner
attached (Draper components
23554 or similar).

■ A tube of solder

Multicore-type non-acid resin.

■ Crocodile clips

Can be used as isolating 'heat sinks' – but not too close to the
joins, as they'll hamper the operation by drawing away too
much heat. A crocodile clip multi-arm is also useful for
holding small components in place.

■ A solder syringe

Makes light work of drawing old solder from previous
electrical joints.

Extra tools for the 'Superstrats'

The Kahler-type fulcrum tremolo fitted to the Japanese
'Standard' requires a Phillips point '1' screwdriver for bridge
height and a 0.050in Allen key for saddle height.

The Washburn Wonder bar requires an 0.050in Allen for
saddle height and rear cam and a ³⁄₃₂in Allen for saddle
intonation pitch change and tremolo spring tension.

The Floyd Rose trem requires a 3mm Hex/Allen for the
locking nut and saddle adjustments.

Useful accessories

- Vaseline or ChapStick for lubrication.
- Silicone or graphite locksmiths' nut lubricant.
- Matchsticks or cocktail sticks for applying lubrication
  and for 'rawlplugging' loose screws.
- Pipe cleaners and cotton buds for cleaning awkward
  spots; an old electric toothbrush can also be useful.
- Radius gauges for setting the bridge saddles.
- An electronic multimeter for testing pickup circuits.
- A set of socket spanners, useful for removing and
  tightening pot nuts, jack sockets, and modern
  machine heads.
- Mechanical and digital callipers – great for all sorts of
  detailed measurements.
- Loctite or similar multi-purpose glue.
- Craft knife for nut work.
- Thread gauges, useful for checking trem arm threads, etc.
- Rubber hammer, safer in many situations when working on
  valuable instruments.
- Wire stripper.
- Lemon oil for rosewood fingerboards.
- Spare jack socket, 250K pot, knobs, and pickup switch.
- Wooden shims for Vintage necks.
- Dental abrasives for fine-tuning a nut slot.

Working environment

Many guitar repairs and much maintenance can be safely
carried out with the guitar resting in its hard shell case on a
normal kitchen table. However, see page 47 on paint repairs for
the precautions that need to be taken against the inhalation of
cellulose etc.

Outside the guitar case environment, a small 1m square of
carpet sample glued to a workbench can avoid a lot of
inadvertent damage to guitar paintwork.

All the guitar techs and luthiers consulted during the writing
of this book seemed to have their own ingenious homemade
tools for very specific jobs.

Essential gig bag accessories

Carrying a few spares can save you a long walk, but you have enough to carry to a gig without hauling your whole toolkit around. The mere essentials compactly rolled in a tool wrap will potentially save a lot of pre-gig hassle, and should fit in your gig bag or guitar case compartment.

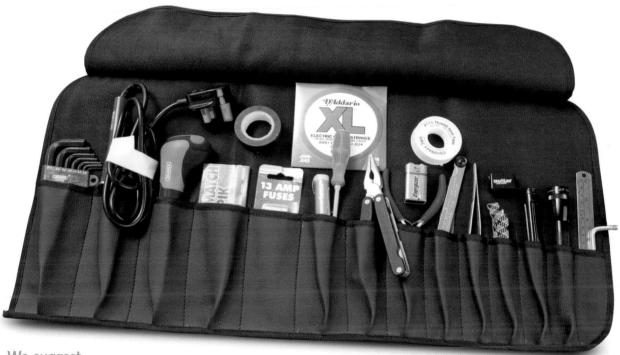

We suggest...

A multipoint screwdriver with Phillips or cross-screw type '0', '1', and '2' point bits and small and medium point conventional heads. (Some very early and many modified Strats are assembled using conventional 'straight' screws as opposed to the more commonly found Phillips variety. A conventional screwdriver is useful to have around anyway, for dealing with broken mains plugs and blown fuses.)

- A small pair of wire snips for emergency string changes.
- Small 'emergency only' soldering iron and 6in of solder.
- Some 13-amp and 5-amp (UK) fuses as well as any specific to your area of touring (ie USA and European equivalents, etc).
- A PP3 battery (for FX).
- A penlight torch.
- Spare plectrums and/or finger picks.

- Allen/Hex keys for loose bridge pieces, etc.
- A nail file.
- Plumbers PTFE tape – very useful as a temporary fix when you lose the tiny tremolo arm tension spring.
- A Leatherman or similar multitool – useful for a sharp blade and decent pliers.
- Capo.
- Insulating tape.
- Feeler gauges.
- A 6in rule.
- An electronic tuner.
- Spare strings.

Unfortunately, by having these with you you'll acquire a reputation as Mr Ever Ready, and before long everybody in the band will come to depend on your tools!

It's worth doing a little maintenance...

...Or getting an expert to do it for you. The Fender Stratocaster is a perfect example of 'the good little runner' – properly 'garaged' and with the minimum of attention it has been known to give good service for over 50 years. Many aficionados reckon the old ones are even better than the new ones. However, the Strat is a mechanical device and even the classiest 1954 two-colour Sunburst will benefit from the occasional minor adjustment. The trick, of course, is to know when to leave well alone.

Vintage antiques

If you are lucky enough to own a '50s Strat then what you have in your possession is not just a good instrument but a piece of popular music history. As such, as well as because of its relative rarity, you must regard the guitar as you would any other valuable 'antique'. Such guitars are considered a valuable investment. I personally share the view of many antique furniture collectors that design and function are part of the charm of such items and therefore they are best kept in use. I hold no truck with the 'investor' who thinks a guitar is best consigned to a bank vault. For me this is missing the point, like the owner who never actually drives his Ferrari. If you check the world's museums you will see that unplayed instruments merely fade and die.

So I recommend you enjoy your guitar whilst observing a few precautions:

■ Never subject the guitar to any extremes of change in temperature and humidity. The chief victim here is the finish, which can crack or 'pave' as the underlying wood shrinks or expands. Vintage type Strats are more prone to this, as their paints and glazes are pervious – which may contribute to the character of their sound as the wood continues to 'breathe'.

■ Give the guitar a good wipe down with a lint-free cloth after playing. This will reduce any damage to metal parts and finish caused by perspiration – the main cause of rust to the bridge and machine heads. This also preserves the strings of course, often doubling their useful life.

■ Keep moving parts suitably lubricated.

■ Use a good, stable guitar stand. This sounds so obvious, but many once-fabulous instruments turn up on the repair bench having been accidentally knocked off some precarious perch.

All those 'hang tags' are worth keeping as they add provenance and value to the guitar.

Authenticity

Many true 'relics' of the '50s have parts missing, knobs and switches particularly. It is perfectly natural to want to replace these and this is completely consistent with Leo Fender's design philosophy. However, it is almost a custodial responsibility to replace them tastefully. These guitars will outlive us and carry on being worthwhile instruments for centuries. I predict the authentic 'early music' enthusiasts of 2050 will include people performing Buddy Holly on authentic '50s Strats with 'tweed' Fender amps. So seek out the most authentic replacement parts possible. It is relatively easy to buy 'aged' plastic parts with a suitable patina that ooze an atmosphere of smoky bars and long years on the chitlin circuit (see *Contacts* in appendix). Do, however, make a careful note of any changes, as this will save argument over authenticity at a later date.

Authenticity remains an issue 'under the hood', and with an old instrument it is extremely prudent to conserve any original cloth-covered wiring and even use authentic '50s-type solders. This may sound over the top at present but the collectors and players of the next century will remember you warmly for taking that extra bit of trouble.

■ Keep the original parts

Over the years I have personally accumulated a small collection of bits from previous guitars, including a couple of bridge parts from a '62 Fiesta Red Strat, my first proper guitar. Now in 1969 when I sold the guitar, these seemed to be scrap metal and it never occurred to me to pass them on. But if the guitar still exists, and it probably does (serial number 87827 – let me know if you have it!), these old parts are an important piece of what antiquarians call 'provenance'. A dealer may spot the 'new' saddle pieces I obtained (with great difficulty) in 1966 and wonder if the guitar really is a '62 Fiesta Red, but if the present owner had the old parts it completes a part of that story which supports the authenticity of the overall instrument. So put those old parts in a safe place and label them with any information you have.

bass that some hooligan had sanded down to the wood but only on the front! I thought that only a complete respray would provide a pleasing finish but John immediately recommended a 'patch'. I was sceptical but on seeing the results I was stunned, the guitar looks wonderful and is still 50 per cent original finish, the odd 'ding' on the original finish gives the guitar a bit of history, but it no longer looks like an industrial accident, which it did before. As a mark of John's true craftsmanship you cannot see the joins. He fastidiously found accurate paints and carefully test-matched the colours, achieving a great result. But this is a drastic step and you wouldn't do it to a Rory Gallagher Strat or a piece of Hendrix kindling wood – that would clearly be erasing history.

Do-it-yourself versus calling in an expert

We all have varying levels of competency in carpentry, electronics and painting. When I obtained my first Strat at the age of 15 it was a complete mess. The teacher I bought it from had bought it on a whim in 1962 at the height of the Shadows' popularity. He learned to play Apache then consigned the guitar to a damp attic. When he retrieved it in 1966, 50 per cent of the metal parts were rusted red to the point where none of the saddles would move and the Klusons had huge gaps in their compliance.

What I did next as an innocent 15-year-old is testament to enthusiasm over experience and serves as a good list of 'do nots':

■ I completely disassembled the guitar, paying no attention to what came from where and in the process lost the carefully-placed neck shims. Take guitars apart carefully and note where everything comes from, especially the screws, which come in many different sizes.

■ I replaced all the rusty screws with the wrong type of replacements. Phillips-type screws were virtually unknown in mid-'60s Britain, but exact Fender replacements are now easily available from many websites (see *Contacts* in appendix).

■ I over-oiled the rusty Klusons thinking they would repair themselves – they didn't, and what's more the excess oil found its way into the neck grain! Again, Kluson replicas are now easily obtained.

■ I replaced the rusty saddles with proper Fender types. These cost a fortune and took six months to arrive from California by ship! Now a websearch would replace them in 48 hours.

When not to respray

Never be tempted to respray a '50s, '60s, or '70s Strat. However tatty it may have become it is worth more in it's original state. Again it's like the 'bruises' on a piece of Chippendale furniture – they are a testimony to the artefact's history. The same, of course, applies to younger Strats, but somehow they don't resonate with quite the same history (yet!).

■ An exception

John Diggins, the brilliant guitar-maker behind the basses of Mark King and the guitars of Tony Iommi, does marvellous 'patch blends' on old finishes. I now think this approach is a good working compromise for newer instruments. A few years ago I presented him with a Sunburst Fender Precision

■ I rewired the electronics to obtain my favourite pickup combinations. Not fatal, but I failed to protect the pickups and capacitors with a heat sink and could have done a lot of damage.

■ I cleaned the volume and tone knobs so well I bleached off the numbers. I replaced a missing knob with a white and gold Fender one – all that Frank Hessy's in Liverpool could offer.

Despite all this the guitar sounded great! I have it on record. However, it was never in tune. The combination of lost neck shims, a poor understanding of the saddle arrangement, rusty Klusons, and a poorly set up tremolo/vibrato meant it drove me nuts – so much so that I sold it for £90 (a fortune in 1969 and a 50 per cent profit on the £60 I paid for it). I don't want to know it's present value, thank you very much.

This book is driven by the desire to help others avoid my youthful errors.

So bottom line, if you are good with tools and prepared to be diligent and extremely careful, you can probably do most of what this manual expounds and either maintain a lovely instrument in peak performance or radically improve an 'economy Strat'.

However, if you have any doubt at all about your abilities call an expert. In 1965 there were no guitar techs (not even for Eric Clapton), only luthiers, who all regarded the Strat as a bit of a joke. Today there are at least half a dozen skilled techs in every major city in the world, and they all have a sneaking regard for the old warhorse that keeps bouncing back.

Never
■ Practice refretting on a vintage instrument. Buy a Squier and learn the craft first.

■ Try to attempt a respray unless you have all the required tools and skills and a dust-free environment. Always wear protective mask and clothing.

■ Force the wrong size screw into a body or component.

■ Always protect the guitar surfaces during any maintenance or lubrication.

But whatever else you do, enjoy that special piece of popular music history by playing it every day and trying very hard to wear it out!

I have seen and played a lot of Stratocasters in the last 40 years and I have this thought to pass on:

A well set up budget Squier is a better working instrument than a poorly set up Custom Shop Eric Clapton. In crude terms a good working Strat is about 70 per cent set-up and 20 per cent the synergy of the parts – all pieces of wood are different and even machined metal parts vary in their composition and microscopic detail. The last 10 per cent is alchemy. Does a guitar respond to being played well? Does the prevalent temperature and humidity affect a guitars sound? Great Strats still have a mystery about them – long may it remain.

✎ Tech Tip

There is no such thing as one perfect set-up – what's right for Mark Knopfler is not right for Eric Clapton – so seek your own ideal set-up.

Glen Saggers – Mark Knopfler's Guitar Tech

Stageside repairs

Given that the electric guitar needs some setting up, it's worth arriving at a gig at least one hour before showtime. This allows for sound-checks and time for the things that go wrong to be put right. Sound-checks give the PA man a chance to serve your needs better – to understand the likely combinations of instruments and any instrument changes during your set. Sound-checks are also great for fault-finding with time to find solutions.

1 No sound from your guitar?

Step 1

■ Work systematically through the cable chain starting at the guitar, as this is very unlikely to have failed completely.

■ Try changing the pickup selector to another pickup. Is the volume control turned up?

■ Still no sound? Try replacing the cable between the guitar and the amplifier with a new cable (one you are sure is working).

■ The above step by passes and eliminates any effects chain.

■ If you have sound, then try re-inserting the effects chain. (Still no sound? Go to Step 2).

■ If you have sound then you merely had a faulty cable, the most common cause of on-stage sound failure.

■ If the sound fails again then it would seem that some component of the effects chain is faulty – work through the chain replacing one cable at a time and hopefully isolating the fault.

■ If cable replacement doesn't solve the problem try systematically removing one effect at a time from the chain.

■ If you find a 'dead' component of the chain try replacing the associated battery or power supply.

Step 2

■ Still no sound, even though you are now plugged directly into the amplifier with a 'new' cable?

■ The likely scenario is a 'failed' amplifier. Try checking the obvious causes, such as:

 – Has the volume been inadvertently turned down to zero?
 – Check the master volume and channel gain.
 – Is the standby switch in the ON position?
 – Does the mains light (if fitted) show 'ON'?
 – Is the amplifier plugged in to the mains? Is the mains switched on? Does the stage have a separate fuse?
 – Are other amplifiers on the same circuit working?

■ If yours is the only failed amp look to the fuses. There are likely to be fuses on the amplifier (usually a screw-type fuse cartridge near the mains switch). There may also be fuses in the mains plug. Try a replacement.

■ If all of this fails to give you sound you must assume the amplifier has a major fault and try a 'work around' it – eg by sharing an amplifier with the other musicians, etc.

■ The crucial thing here is to be systematic – work through the chain logically, eliminating elements of the chain until the fault is isolated.

2 The guitar won't stay in tune?

Strings!

The most likely cause of tuning difficulties on an otherwise well maintained guitar is poor or worn strings. The bad news is that changing strings one hour before a gig is also a formula for disaster, as the strings really need time to settle. In an emergency try replacing any individual strings that seem particularly troublesome – rusty first second and third strings will inevitably cause severe tuning problems.

Loose components?

■ Have the neck securing screws worked loose?

■ Are the machine heads or string tree loose?

NB: A machine head that is securely fitted but turns without altering pitch needs replacement. In practice this is unlikely to happen suddenly and should be picked up during routine maintenance.

■ Is the tremolo/vibrato unit poorly set up? This is unlikely to respond to a quick fix *see 'Trem alignment' page 39*, but in an emergency a 'blocked off' tremolo may provide a temporary solution. *See 'Hard Tail options' page 78*.

In practice any loose component in the string path will cause instability and hence tuning problems – examine the guitar for loose screws and lost or corroded securing springs. If the strings are OK and there are no obvious loose components then perhaps you have changed string gauges without realigning the guitar?

Three-monthly checks

The Stratocaster guitar was designed by a man and a team who were either musicians or knew musicians well. They knew the guitar needed to be low maintenance, and by and large it is. The Stratocaster will even survive neglect and abuse. In his 'demolition' period Pete Townshend of The Who once complained that Strats were hard to break! Jimi Hendrix famously torched his at Monterey, but even that guitar recently came up for sale at Sotheby's.

However, most of us want our Strat to last and to perform consistently well. The guitar will play better in response to a little care and attention.

Strings

Change these according to use, at least weekly if you're a gigging professional and at least every three months for students. Use the same brand consistently and use the same gauge and metal type, as this will save time-consuming adjustments to the action and intonation. Different strings have different tensions and gauges can vary from heavy to extra light. Cheap strings are generally a false economy – they are inconsistent and wear out quicker.

A good 'benchmark' in stringing a modern Strat is 009 (first) to 042 (sixth) – light gauge strings for flexibility, but not too light. Experiment around this area for your own sound. Hank Marvin of the British group The Shadows achieved his distinctive early sound with much heavier strings – but that was in an era before much 'string bending' activity.

More recently Stevie Ray Vaughan has used heavier strings to achieve a distinctive tone (he managed to 'bend' his heavy strings by tuning them below standard concert pitch). Some heavy metal and 'shred' guitarists use strings lighter than 009. Experiment, but refer to *'Set up and tuning' page 30* in this manual to ensure your guitar is adjusted to cope.

New strings are consistent in their profile and hence more harmonically correct along their length – this makes them easier to tune. Old strings are worn by fret contact, are inconsistent, and above all sound dull.

Keep new strings sounding good longer by wiping them after every use with a lint-free cloth. This removes corrosive perspiration and prevents premature rusting.

Early Strats came fitted with burnished strings and some players even fitted flat-wound strings of a type more usually associated with mainstream jazz styles. Today's fashionable guitar sounds tend to be bright and crisp and this is best achieved with conventional round-wound strings, usually made of nickel wound on steel. Stainless steel is another long-lasting option, though beware of using strings that are made of a material harder than your frets, as inevitably this will result in quicker fret wear.

'Coated strings' are more resistant to corrosion though initially more expensive.

Always use electric guitar strings. This sounds obvious, but acoustic guitar strings are not designed for magnetic pickups and are therefore not always magnetically consistent – electric strings are! Stick to one brand as these will be balanced across the gauges, both physically and magnetically. If you want to hear the results of acoustic strings on an electric guitar listen to the 1946 Django Reinhardt sessions – even Django struggled to get a consistent response.

To reduce string breakage lubricate the string/saddle contact point with a light machine oil (3-in-1 oil contains anti-rust and anti-corrosive properties). Do this every time you change your strings. The oil acts as an insulator against moisture, and reduces friction and metal fatigue.

Another area that should be lubricated is the string tree(s). A small amount of ChapStick, applied with a matchstick, will suffice.

Stringing a Strat – vintage keys
These feature a unique slotted barrel.

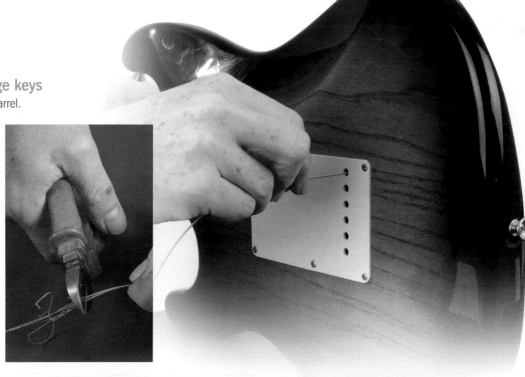

One obstacle to changing Vintage Strat strings is the 'thru body' stringing. However, if the trem is aligned properly then it shouldn't be too difficult – the trem block holes should line up with the holes in the plastic back plate *see 'Trem alignment' page 39.*

■ When removing old strings, cutting off the curly ends will assist their passage through the trem block.

1 When possible always change one string at a time to avoid drastic changes in tension on the neck and vibrato assembly.
Due to the unique Vintage design you will need to pre-cut the strings to achieve the proper length and the desired amount of winds.
Starting with the sixth string first, pull the new sixth string (taking up any slack) to the fourth key (this will give you enough length for the windings).

■ Bend and crimp the string to a 90° angle…

…and cut it to length.

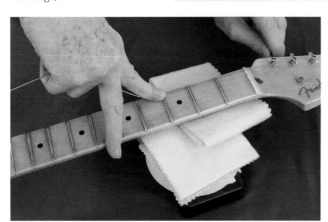

2 Insert the string into the centre hole in the tuning key, and wind neatly in a downward pattern – carefully, so as to prevent overlapping the windings. Keep the string under tension with your fingers.

3 Repeat the procedure as above, ie pull the fifth string to the third key and cut and tension it. Then pull the fourth string between the second and first keys and cut it. Pull the third string just about to the top of the headstock and cut it. Pull the second string about 0.5in (13mm) past the headstock and cut it. Finally, pull the first string 1.5in (38mm) past the top of the headstock and cut it.

Stringing a Strat – standard keys

Many 'modern' Strats have a conventional horizontal hole in the machine head barrel.

NB: If your tuning keys have a screw on the end of the button, check the tightness of the screw, as this controls the tension of the gears inside the tuning keys. You should slacken this tension for ease of re-stringing. After stringing it is very important not to over-tighten these screws. They should be tightened only 'finger-tight'. This is particularly important on locking tuners.

1 In order to reduce string slippage at the tuning key, I recommend that you use a tie technique. This is accomplished by pulling the string through the keyhole, then pulling it clockwise underneath itself and bringing it back over the top of itself, creating a knot.

This is done under tension and achieves a situation with very few turnings on the machine head barrel. This is particularly desirable when extensive use is made of the trem – less windings mean less 'unwindings' as the trem is depressed and the string tension reduced.

You'll need to leave a bit of slack for the first string, so you have perhaps two to three winds around the post. As you progress down the line to the sixth string you'll reduce the amount of slack and the amount of winds around the keys.

2 Tighten the string under tension as above.

3 Crimp the excess string with wire cutters.

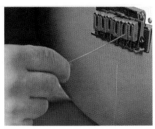

■ Johns cake tester in use!

Fender recommendations

For tuning stability Fender recommend Fender Bullet strings.

The patented bullet-end is specifically designed for all styles of Fender tremolo/vibrato use, from extreme 'dives' to smooth vibrato passages. The design allows the string to travel freely in the bridge block channel during tremolo use and return afterwards to its original position, seated snugly in the bridge block. This is accomplished by eliminating the extra string wrap and the ball-end (a conventional ball-end doesn't quite fit properly in the Strat string channel). The 'bullet-end' has been shaped and sized to precisely match the design of the bridge block channel.

However, the bullets – and indeed, sometimes conventional 'ball ends' too – can become lodged in their sockets in the trem block.

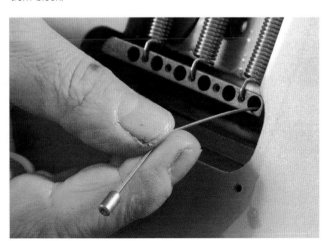

String stretching

To avoid slippage stretch your strings properly. Having installed a new set and tuned them to pitch, hold the strings at the first fret and hook your fingers under each string (one at a time) and tug lightly, moving your hand from the bridge to the neck. Re-tune the guitar and repeat this process several times.

Check for corrosion

The bridge assembly on Vintage-type Strats can easily become damaged by perspiration. This sometimes causes the adjustment screws to lock solid – avoid this by cleaning regularly with a small amount of lighter fuel on a Q-Tip or Baby Bud.

Be careful when doing this to avoid misaligning the length and height adjustment screws. Always dry the bridge after playing with a clean lint-free cloth. See below for lubrication recommendations.

Machine heads require similar checks and are naturally prone to perspiration corrosion.

Jack socket

Heavy use may result in electrical 'crackling'. If this is the case try adjusting the tension on the spring steel jack retainer.

1 Remove the retaining screws and carefully remove the jack socket from its moulded seating. A jackplug secured in the jack socket will provide a useful extraction tool.

On a valuable instrument take care to protect the guitar paintwork with a duster taped in place with low adhesion masking tape.

2 A gentle squeeze of the spring steel jack retainer may restore the required electrical contact sufficiently.

■ If the jack socket seems beyond repair then consider fitting an approved Fender replacement. This may be a little more expensive than a cheap jack socket from a radio repair shop but it will be the right size and is likely to be more suitably robust. All jack sockets are not created equal.

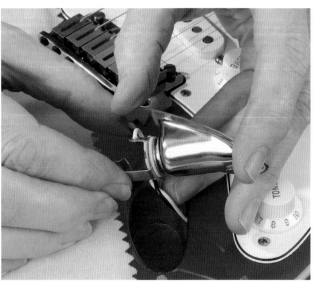

3 Replacement (if required). If in any doubt label the cables as 'tip' and 'sleeve'. Then carefully melt the solder joins and remove the old jack socket.

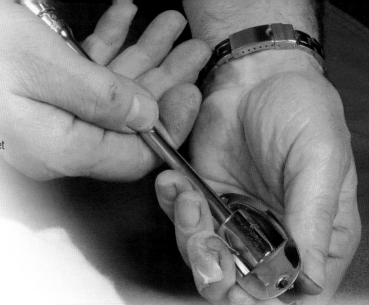

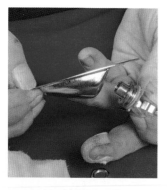

4 Remove the jack socket from the moulded chrome retainer by unscrewing the nut.

■ You can find the correct socket size by trial and error or refer to the appropriate case studies in this book for guidance.

5 Solder the new jack socket, retaining the tip and sleeve polarity as per your labelling. NB: Use .32in 60/40 Rosin Core electrical solder and a pen-type iron rated at 25W and above.

6 Re-bolt the jack socket in position and refit the chrome retainer.

Frets

Examine your frets. Check for wear by gently moving the strings aside from their normal fret position.

Slight and even wear should not be a problem, but any badly 'grooved' frets need to be monitored and if necessary replaced. *See 'Fret Polish' page 65 and case study 'Chinese Squier' page 146.*

Machine heads

Check for loose machine-head retaining screws and tighten if necessary with a number '0' or '1'Phillips type screwdriver.

More importantly, check for 'dead spots' in the machine head mechanism – that is to say, spots in the turn where no pitch-change is heard in the relevant string. This is an indicator of wear on the machine-head gears. These are 'lifetime lubricated' and oiling them is best avoided.

Vintage Strats have machine heads by Kluson, and Fender replaced these with Kluson lookalikes in 1967. Later Strats have Schaller-made machine heads labelled as 'Fender' – both types are readily available (see *Contacts* in appendix). A third type of Vintage tuner is made by Gotoh (Japan). These were introduced in 1981. If replacement is necessary see *Machine head replacement.*on page 38

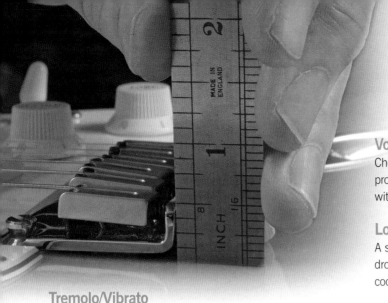

Tremolo/Vibrato

Check the angle between the body and bridge assembly. This should be ⅛in (nominal).

The trem should be silent in operation, with no 'spring pings'. For adjustment and lubrication *see 'Trem alignment and lubrication' page 39*.

Fingerboard wear

Check for fingerboard wear. Superficial removal of the fingerboard lacquer common on maple boards, as illustrated, is not in itself a problem. More worrying is the appearance of dips or grooves in the wood itself – this requires attention. *See 'Paint and lacquer repairs' page 70*.

Action

Check the action height with a car feeler gauge (.002–.025), applying Fender recommended specifications:

Neck radius	String height Bass side	String height Treble side
7.25in	¾₄in/.7081in	¾₄in/¹⁄₆in/.0625in
9.5in to 12in	¾₄in	¾₄in
15in to 17in	¾₄in	¾₄in/.0469in

For details of your specific Stratocaster neck radius refer to the case studies section of this book.

If the action is too high or two low, *see 'Setting up and tuning' page 30*.

Volume and tone controls

Check these for electrical crackles and 'dead spots'. If these problems are present then the pots may respond to a treatment with switch cleaner. *See 'Volume controls' page 85*.

Loose strap retainers

A simple problem that can cause havoc if the guitar is eventually dropped! If the retaining screw is loose when fully tightened a cocktail stick or split matchstick will usually work as a rawlplug.

Pingy strings?

Check for a pinging noise whilst tuning each individual string. If present this is often due to the string sticking in the nut grooves at the top of the neck. A light lubrication of graphite dust or silicone projected into the grooves will usually solve this annoying problem and even help tuning stability.

Lubrication

One of the most important elements in ensuring tuning stability and reducing string breakage is lubricating all of the contact points of a string's travel. This particularly applies when heavy use is made of the vibrato/tremolo.

Graphite applied to nut groove.

Sometimes a simple pencil will suffice.

A fret polish

Budget Strats often arrive with rather unfinished frets. They are workable but feel a little rough, especially when 'bending' strings. The solution is a little simple polishing.

1 After removing the strings mask the fretboard with some masking tape.

2 Wearing protective gloves and eye protection, carefully dress the frets with some 000 grade wire wool. Beware of overdoing this, as you can change the shape of the frets and cause much worse problems. Remove the masking tape

3 A light application of a little lemon oil will restore the finish on a rosewood fingerboard and also help remove any adhesive deposit left by the tape.

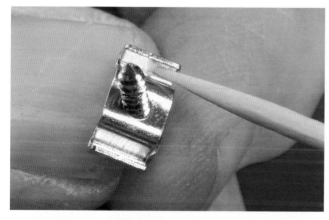

String breakage

The foremost contributor to this is moisture collection at the point of contact on the bridge saddle. This can be attributed to the moisture and acidity that transfers from your hands or can be a direct effect of humidity in the air.

■ Metal conflict

Metal-to-metal friction and fatigue is a scientific fact that affects any mechanical device employing a combination of metal materials.

Different metal components, in contact over a period of time, react to each other and breakdown the integrity of, for instance, guitar strings. A stronger metal will always attack a softer metal (this is why a stainless-steel string may wear a groove into a vintage-style saddle). Finally, you will also find that different string brands will break at different points of tension, due to the metal make-up and string manufacturing techniques.

One of the ways to reduce string breakage is to lubricate the string/saddle contact point with a light machine oil (3-in-1 oil, which also contains anti-rust and anti-corrosive properties is ideal). The oil acts not only as an insulator against moisture, but also reduces friction and metal fatigue. This lubrication needs to be done sparingly. Use a matchstick or 'Q'-tip end to transfer a minimum of oil to each saddle.

For the string tree, a small amount of ChapStick or Vaseline, applied with a cocktail stick, works wonders.

Earthing and RF induction issues

The electric guitar and particularly the single coil pickup variety, can be prone to a lot of 'Rattle and Hum'. There are steps that can be taken to improve matters.

The historical perspective

In 1952–3 when Leo and his colleagues designed the Strat, the venues their customers were playing were bars, lounges, and small dance halls. Early Strat users such as Howlin' Wolf were playing in small clubs with no dedicated PA system and no stage lighting. In these conditions an electrically unscreened and 'unbalanced' single coil pickup was no real problem. If the player heard a little hum from his amp he could just shift around a little until his pickup was 'off axis' to the radio frequencies emanating from his valve amps' huge transformers. Potential radio interference was confined to the output from a few local and national stations.

By 1957 this situation had changed, as early Strat adopters like Buddy Holly might play theatres and even some television shows. The lighting dimmers in such situations often induced a lot of hum into audio circuits via the unbalanced unscreened pickups, and not just at the low 50–60Hz frequencies that were easily 'lost in the mix'. Soon audience were hearing nasty 'spikes' in the vocal frequencies – which happens to be the audio range where our ears are most sensitive.

The early PA pioneers (of which Leo was one) were naturally inclined to solve the problem by utilising 'balanced' line audio circuits with their 'humbucking' properties, but guitarists were left with a growing noise problem.

Today popular music of all kinds has gravitated to stadiums and auditoria bristling with hundreds of computer-programmed lighting dimmers, electric server-driven lighting changes, electrical smoke machines, radio microphones, intercoms, mobile phones and millions of watts of amplification putting every tiny buzz and hum under a microscope. As if this were not enough there are now, of course, thousands of radio transmissions, legal and illegal, all of which can sometimes mistake your guitar and amplifier for a radio receiver.

Humbucking guitar pickups are a part solution, but they do have a different sound. Many guitarists prefer the classic character of electrically 'unbalanced' single coil pickups. In search of a solution, Leo started experimenting with 'screened' metal laminated pickguards for the Strat as early as 1960. He had even tried gold anodised metal pickguards as early as 1954 (on Dave Gilmour's Strat 0001).

The screening concept is to build a metallic shield around sensitive 'unbalanced' guitar circuits and connect this 'screen' to an earth potential. The screen effectively intercepts any interference – noise – and drains it away to earth before it can affect the signal passing along the guitar circuits.

Supplementary screening

One part solution suggested by guitar craftsman John Diggins is a screening paint, applied in the pickup cavities. John specifically recommends carbon graphite paint but also advises that it won't completely solve the problem in today's increasingly electronically 'busy' world.

SAFETY FIRST: Always use a vapour-barrier facemask/respirator and eye protection when applying specialist paints.

1 Remove the guitar strings and carefully remove the covers from all the cavities you intend to screen. Keep all the screws together in a series of pots and trays – it's worth labelling these NOW, as putting the wrong screws back in the wrong holes will inevitably cause problems.

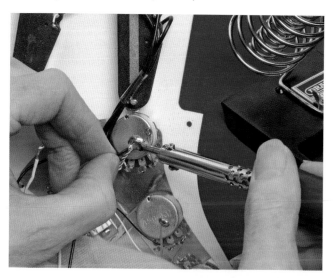

2 Carefully unsolder the electrical connections and label the cables for ease of re-installation. It's probably worth drawing a simple diagram to remind yourself of what came from where.

3 Carefully prepare the surfaces for painting, removing any grease or rough woodwork that may hamper the adhesion of the paint.

4 Apply the first coat of paint, and allow this to dry

WARNING: This paint will be a very effective conductor, so be careful to only apply it where a route to earth or ground is desirable. A bit of paint in the wrong place, which on reassembly touches a 'hot' wire, can short circuit the guitar.

5 Affix a copper strip to the cavity, located at a point where this will contact the existing screening plate when the guitar is reassembled, effectively forming an electrical continuity to earth via the jack socket and your guitar lead.

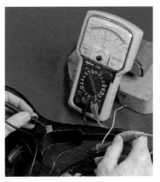

6 Apply a second coat of the screening paint. A second coat will invariably improve the effectiveness and continuity of the new screen.

When dry, check for continuity of the 'circuit' created by your new screen. The easiest way to do this is by placing your multimeter prongs at several spaced points on the finish and checking the continuity you've achieved.

7 If necessary solder a wire from your new screen to the earth side of your jack socket. The need for this will depend on the extent of your painting and whether or not the paint is going to contact an existing earth point on reassembly.

Another part solution to noise induction

A second suggestion from John Diggins is to wire the middle pickup in the opposite polarity, 'effectively making a noise-cancelling pair when two pickups are engaged together'. This, of course, has an impact on the combined sound, which you may or may not prefer. As a point of fact Fender now do this on most of their Strat models except the Vintage Reissues (according to George Blanda, one of the men behind the American Standard).

Guitar leads as aerials

As well as noise induced into the pickups guitarists have increasingly long guitar leads to contend with. A long length of 'unbalanced' guitar lead can act as a giant aerial, picking up all sorts of electrical noise and radio frequencies (RF), all of which will be amplified just as effectively as any audio signal running down the line. We've all been to a gig where you suddenly hear taxi radios and ambulance messages blaring through the PA. This is usually the result of RF picked up by unbalanced guitar pick-ups or leads. Better screening can sometimes help.

8 Carefully reassemble the pickguard/pickup assembly, checking for all points of contact with the new screened surface. All pickups and potentiometers (volume/tone) and switches must be clear of contact with the new surface. When soldering, a dab of 'tinner cleaner' RS 561 533 will improve the conductivity of the solder iron heat and aid a quicker, more effective solder joint.

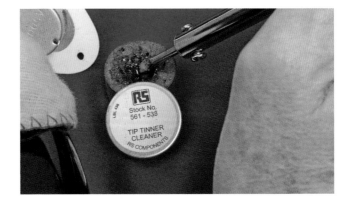

Mains hum

In order to reduce 50–60Hz mains hum from induction, it's very important to route all your audio cables (guitar FX and microphones) physically away from the mains cables from your gear, as well as elements such as power amplifiers and external power supplies (wall warts). A good rule of thumb is, when an audio cable has to cross the path of a mains cable, make sure it crosses at a right angle – this minimises the induction of this type of hum.

Earth loops

An even more common source of hum is the infamous earth loop, also known as a 'ground loop'. These are often difficult to track down and isolate. However, once you've applied most of the common-sense measures to reduce hum, any hum remaining will usually be attributable to an earth loop. It is possible to completely eliminate earth loops if you take the necessary steps, but it involves a systematic process of eliminating problems one component at a time.

■ So What Is an Earth Loop?

Earth loops occur because most modern equipment is fitted with three-pin mains plugs. The third pin on the plug connects the chassis of your gear to AC earth, which ensures that your body cannot become the earth path for AC current. All well and good.

However, when two pieces of equipment both have three-pin plugs and are connected together with cable, the shielding on the cable is also responsible for 'grounding', and an earth loop is possible.

What we now have is two paths to earth (one through it's own AC cable; the other through the audio cable connected to the other unit, and consequently through that unit's AC cable). Thus a loop of current is formed that can act like an aerial, perfect for inducing hum. You can even pick up radio interference this way, as you have effectively created a 'tuned circuit'. If you were doing this on purpose you would call it a radio, but Marconi beat you to it!

■ Troubleshooting

Most earth loop problems can be solved by plugging all of your stage gear into a single earthed AC outlet. However, it's easily possible to overload the AC outlet, so make sure the AC source is rated to handle all the gear you have plugged into it. A guitar amp itself and a couple of FXs will certainly be less than the UK standard 13 amps, but beware of plugging the whole band into one socket! And remember that different countries have different standards or ratings for AC outlets. It's in the interests of your safety to know these.

The only way of being sure you have a potential earth loop problem is to listen carefully for a slightly edgy hum as you're assembling, wiring, and cabling your system. Have your gear powered and monitor for hum after each audio connection. This way you can quickly determine and isolate the source of the problem.

Once you identify the unit that is causing the hum you have to find a 'work around'. This may mean a compromise on the number and position of the units in your audio chain.

It's worth physically moving the unit that seems to be causing the problem and trying again. Sometimes the close proximity of items such as mains transformers can be aggravating the induction problem. You can eliminate battery-operated gear, or gear with two-prong adaptors, as they cannot contribute to earth loop problems.

■ Earth Lift

Some people solve earth loop problems by using a 'lifting' device (three-prong to two-prong adaptor) on one of the units, thus breaking the earth route and severing the loop.

However, NB: This is a very dangerous option that should not be used. You are negating the safety factor that the AC earth wire provides. If you choose to use three-to two-prong AC adaptors, electrocution may result.

■ Isolating Transformers

The best (but more expensive) way to fix a persistent earth loop problem is through the use of a transformer. The job of the transformer is to ensure there is no electrical contact between two pieces of equipment, except for the audio signal. Transformers have no earth connection between the input and output connections, thus effectively breaking an earth loop.

When buying transformers for earth loop problems, it's important to realise that the cheaper variety may colour the sound a little due to frequency response irregularities. Buy the best you can afford – it's worth it.

Intermittents

In my experience these are the worst sort of interference, as you're never sure if they're 'cured'.

If you hear a buzz that only appears for a short time and at a constant level, you may have a pulse in your mains lines, which can be caused by the switching action of fluorescent lighting, dimmer switches, window air conditioners, or a refrigerator turning on and off. Again it's a matter of working through the possibilities in a systematic way.

If you must share an AC circuit with any of these elements, and if it's a long-term gig, somebody needs to install a proprietary noise-suppressed AC distribution panel, which will give you a clean power supply for your stage.

Paint and lacquer repairs

As the Stratocaster has shifted position from a disposable working man's guitar to a collectable style icon, a dilemma has arisen over paintwork and lacquer repairs. I will state quite clearly from the beginning that no amateur would be wise to set about finish repairs on a rare and valuable guitar.

John Diggins is a first rate craftsman luthier who could build you a Fender Stratocaster from scratch starting from bare hunks of timber. His workshop is perfumed by the smell of swamp ash and nitrocellulose. He has 30 years of experience to draw on following an apprenticeship with legendary luthier John Birch.

Even John is loath to mess with guitars that have seen a bit of gigging. However, what I presented him was a very nicely looked-after reproduction '57 Fiesta Red Vintage Reissue from 1996 (my own guitar!). Despite my admiration for John's work I did this with some trepidation. I have owned the guitar for about six years and it's been quietly gigged and played every day. It's a first-rate guitar, the best Strat I've ever played, and it is very stable, mostly due to a brilliant set-up by guitar tech Stuart Monks of Peter Cook's Guitars, Hanwell, London.

The repairs below were largely driven by necessity – I had worn away a lot of the polyurethane on the fingerboard and was beginning to wear away the maple.

The body lacquer repairs were largely cosmetic. I resented the ding on the lower bout, as it wasn't done by me. The flaking lacquer on the neck socket was getting worse every day and seemed a pity to tolerate on an otherwise very 'clean' guitar.

What follows is a 'my documentary' of John's approach to dealing with these two challenges.

Fingerboard wear on a ten-year-old guitar. This is starting to affect the wood itself and needs attention.

Re-lacquering a maple neck

1 Remove the strings. John is always keen to avoid shocks to the wood and removes strings the old-fashioned way, one string at a time

2 Remove the machine heads with a '1' point Phillips screwdriver. John uses small plastic trays to retain the original screws and parts.

3 Loosen the frets with a hammer and chisel (I couldn't look!). Note the use of a neck cradle.

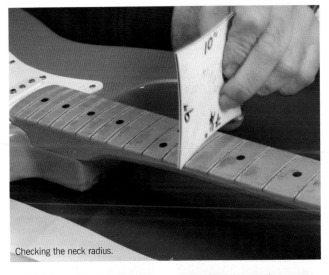

Checking the neck radius.

4 Carefully prise the frets out with razor sharp custom ground end cutters – the frets are not badly worn and will be replaced in the neck after refinishing the fingerboard. John kept a careful record of the fret order by assembling them on a piece of gaffer tape.

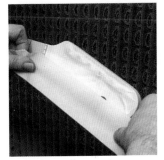

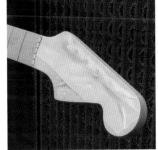

5 Remove the neck using a '2' point Phillips screwdriver. John was careful to check for any shims in the neck socket – in this case there were none, which suggests the guitar was accurately made at the outset.

6 It was decided to leave the front of the headstock intact as this has the '50s Fender 'Spaghetti' transfer and the 'contour body' logo. So low-adhesion masking tape was carefully applied and trimmed.

7 Placing the neck in a wooden carpenters' vice, John began the task of carefully removing the polyurethane from the remainder of the neck and fingerboard. He used a carefully selected sanding block with a 7.25in radius in order to retain the fingerboard shape. The abrasive is light grade P80 3M255, working up to even lighter 180 grit for the finish.

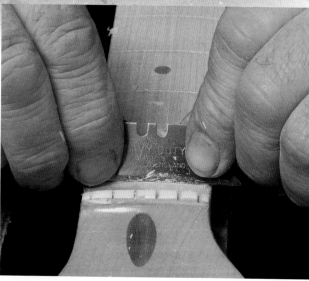

8 In order to trim the polyurethane precisely to the nut John employs a Stanley craft knife blade as a fine scraper.

9 John had to take off quite a lot of wood to even out the fingerboard indentations, so this meant restoring the depth of the fret slots with a special custom width fret saw.

10 The fingerboard is then finished with 000 grade wire wool.

11 John constantly checks for a flat, even fingerboard using a straight edge held up to the light.

12 Turning the neck over, John uses a custom-made jig that utilises the truss rod thread for a securing bolt. This enables access to the complete neck surface.

13 Another two custom-shaped scrapers are utilised to evenly bare the nooks and crannies of the rear of the maple neck.

14 Again, the whole is finished with 80 and 180 grade 3M TRI-M-ITE FRECUT abrasive – NOT glasspaper. The final finish is again achieved with 000 grade wire wool.

15 The neck is mounted in a custom-made revolving jig within a dust-free and extractor-fan equipped spray booth. The revolve enhances an even spray and the extractors protect John's lungs and control dust – the biggest enemy of a clear spray finish.

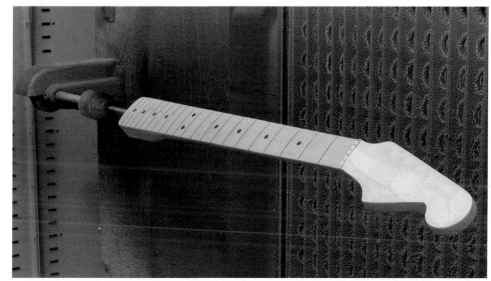

16 The nitrocellulose base coat is applied using a fine spray on the revolving neck. This is allowed to dry for several hours.

17 A rub down with 400 grit abrasive achieves a key for the second base coat. This is applied and allowed to dry.

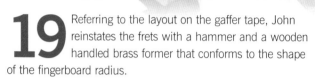

18 The final coat of a darker 'pre-aged' nitrocellulose is applied using a specially designed (pre-CBS) mustard jar spray container. The neck now looks fantastic and is put in a special drying cupboard overnight.

19 Referring to the layout on the gaffer tape, John reinstates the frets with a hammer and a wooden handled brass former that conforms to the shape of the fingerboard radius.

20 A diamond stone is used to dress the edges of the frets.

21 Any burrs are removed using a 2mm radius fret file – all without damaging the new nitrocellulose!

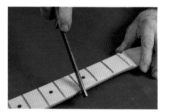

22 The machine heads are reinstalled in random order apart from the two end machines, which are 'position critical'. A '1' point Phillips screwdriver avoids screw head damage. Note John has not obscured the dating information on the neck heel.

23 Having reinstated the string tree, the neck is ready for reinstalling on the body.

Bodywork repairs

1 A light abrasive is used to prepare the surfaces and provide a key.

2 The 'ding' is filled with cellulose filler, allowed to dry, and abraded to a finish.

3 The areas are sprayed in a dust-proof environment using a tiny modellers' spray. The Fiesta Red lacquer is authentically hand-mixed from base colours. In John's experience no two Fiesta Reds are identical due to paint batch variations, ageing, and the effects of ultraviolet and smoke. He colour matched the finish by eye!

4 John hand-finished the edges of the new lacquer with a fine camelhair brush and allowed the finish to dry for several hours.

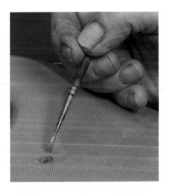

5 A polish with a gentle cutting paste helped integrate the new lacquer.

6 The finished repair blends extremely well.

7 The neck and body are reassembled using a '2' point Phillips – these neck 'bolts' need to be firmly tightened and any shims need to be reinstated. I like the way the retouch looks the correct colour but doesn't look 'new'.

'String Guide' variants

From its very inception the Fender guitar was different! Virtually every other guitar ever made up until 1948 had a headstock that angled back away from the nut. This convention ensured downward pressure on the nut, which both kept the strings in place and ensured a good tone.

Leo's was different. His 'working man's' guitar would be lean, mean, and efficient. Curiously his innovation saves wood, which is good for productivity and also for the environment. Having saved some wood and created a distinctive and very different headstock (based, he says, on some Croatian guitars he'd seen*), Leo was left with a problem, which he solved for the 'Broadcaster' guitar in 1950 by introducing a round string guide to pull the first and second strings in towards the neck. This round string guide is still found on some very early Strats but is more often replaced by a custom-made 'string tree', which does the same job.

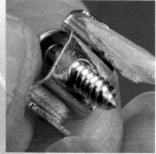

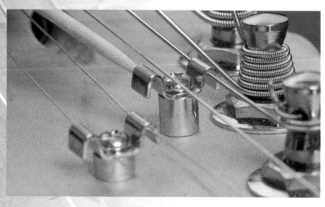

■ The slightest touch of lubrication here (using Lipsalve, ChapStick, or Vaseline) will avoid any 'sticking' causing intonation problems. This particularly applies when heavy use is made of the vibrato/tremolo arm.

*The Croatian guitars still used in Istria have this distinctive Stauffer type of headstock, but I'm not sure of how Stauffer links with Istria, though I suspect the link is Istria's cultural links with Venice.

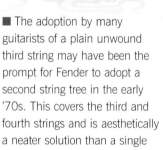

■ The adoption by many guitarists of a plain unwound third string may have been the prompt for Fender to adopt a second string tree in the early '70s. This covers the third and fourth strings and is aesthetically a neater solution than a single or triple 'tree'.

American Series 2000 onwards

A third option found on the American Series Strats which replaced the American Standard in 2000, features a neat combination of a low friction 'roller' type string tree for the first and second strings combined with staggered lower string posts for the top four strings. This is an effective solution to the 'nut tension' issue.

■ Exception

The string tree would only be an encumbrance on any of the 'Superstrats' that incorporate roller bridges, such as 2002's American Deluxe Fat Strat or Richie Sambora's locking trem Signature guitar. Naturally the locking bar of a Floyd Rose ensures plenty of downward pressure at the nut. See *Mexican Fat Strat* on page 118. The latest Strats have staggered tuner pegs to assist with correct nut angle issues – and so the evolution continues.

Very occasionally string trees may have been positioned incorrectly at the factory. This means that the desirable 'straight pull' which Leo intended is distorted. Remedying this without leaving unsightly holes in the headstock is a job for a well-equipped and skilled luthier.

✎ Tech Tip

The extra string tree helps when an inexperienced player replacing his strings doesn't allow enough windings on the string post, leaving a fairly gentle slope up to the nut – the string spacer provides the necessary pressure at the nut.

Andy Gibson of London's Tin Pan Alley

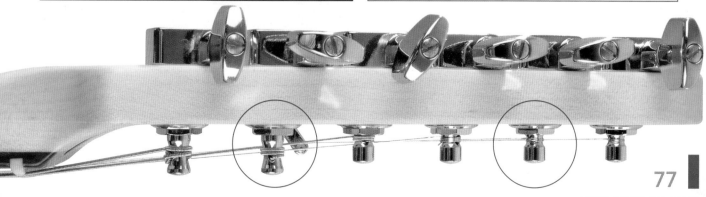

'Hard Tail' options

When Leo and his colleagues designed the Stratocaster they were improving what they called 'The Fender guitar', and the addition of a vibrato/tremolo mechanism took them nearer to their ideal of a guitar that sounded closer to a steel or Hawaiian guitar. This would better serve their 'Western Swing' customers. It also worked brilliantly for instrumental bands such as The Ventures in the USA and The Shadows in the UK, who quickly developed a whole new technique built on the creative use of the 'Vibrato'.

Their guitars, like every other guitar of that era, were strung with medium or heavy gauge strings, and the use of string 'bending' techniques to achieve a portamento effect was not only rare but also – with such heavy strings – difficult.

The development of urban blues in Chicago in the '50s and '60s found Buddy Guy and his contemporaries experimenting with the new Fender guitars and stringing them with much lighter strings to better facilitate 'string bending' for portamento effects. It's thought this may have been seen as an alternative to using the 'bottleneck' technique common in acoustic country blues.

As light gauge strings were not yet commercially available players often substituted a light gauge banjo G string for the E first string and used the E string as a second string. The B string became the first unwound 'plain' third, replacing the then normal wound third, which became the new fourth, and so on. Country music players in Nashville adopted the same modification and for a period the string substitution was commonly referred to as 'Nashville stringing'.

When you use string bending techniques with a standard Fender 'synchronised tremolo'/vibrato there is a natural tendency for the whole 'floating bridge' assembly to move, effectively cancelling some of the string bending effect and also detuning all the other 'unbent' strings. Though this didn't bother Jimi Hendrix or Jeff Beck, who both utilised the effect as part of their style, it doesn't appeal to everyone.

Several players devised homemade solutions to this issue. Screwing the bridge hard down to the body is one of them, and blocking the tremolo string block with a piece of wood is another.

Fender realised some players wanted a 'hard tail' version of the Strat and offered one as an ex-factory item as early as April 1955. However, this option has never proved very popular. It would seem quite logical that the metal of the trem block and even the trem springs must contribute something to the distinctive Strat sound. For example, the Eric Clapton Signature model has a blocked-off trem, though Eric never uses it, so he clearly feels the mechanism is worth retaining for its secondary tonal effect.

Do-It-Yourself 'Hard Tail'

1 Remove the strings one at a time, working from the outer two inwards – ie first and sixth, then second and fifth, then third and fourth. This will avoid putting the guitar neck through any sudden changes in tension and will mean less resetting.

2 Carefully remove the plastic backplate from the tremolo/vibrato cavity using a Phillips '1' point screwdriver.

3 Check which kind of trem block is fitted to your guitar – this could be a classic '50s and '60s style solid steel block or a much lighter and tapered cast alloy block as found on Squiers.

4 Carefully measure the cavity – a vernier gauge is ideal for this.

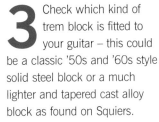

5 From a small scrap of hardwood, fashion a custom block to fit the tapers inside the cavity behind the existing metal tremolo block. This will be approximately 0.5in/12mm thick by 3in/7.5cm long by as much as 1.75in/4cm deep, though you should rough-cut it slightly oversize and custom sand it for a snug fit. The John Diggins example illustrated is actually quite small but effective.

6 With the trem springs as a grip, the new hardwood block should hold itself snugly in position.

NB: At least one of the trem springs should be left in place, as this provides earth or ground continuity via the wiring to the spring 'claw'. As they contribute to the sound they are best all left in place – Eric Clapton has five in the back of his 'hard tail'.

7 Replace the plastic tremolo backplate. You may want to consider replacing the cover with the latest Fender American Series type. This has larger access holes for stringing and the metal vibrato block may now be otherwise difficult to access in its new blocked-off position.

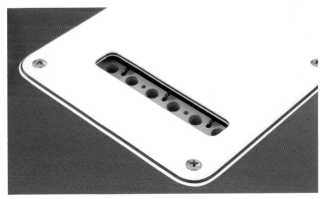

Pickup replacement

Arguably the most potent aspect of the Strat's sound is its single coil pickups with alnico magnets.

Superficially all single coil Strat-type pickups may look the same, but a closer look reveals many subtle and some not so subtle variations.

As the case studies in this book reveal, pickup outputs can vary, and different types of coil windings, wire thicknesses etc all have a significant effect on the crucial sound.

Many cheap Strats – particularly the Chinese-made Squier 'Affinity' – have cost-efficient but (some would suggest) 'sound compromised' pickup arrangements. Consequently the most common 'improvement' to a basic Strat is a pickup replacement. There are many replacement pickup options, but as we're dealing with the Fender guitar I will detail the most popular change, which entails fitting Fender Texas Specials to a budget Squier guitar. These slightly overwound pickups are based on those used by Stevie Ray Vaughan and feature in the SRV Fender guitar.

The replacement pickups are available from Fender dealers and come as a matched set of three, complete with all the wiring, screws, and pickup covers you're likely to need.

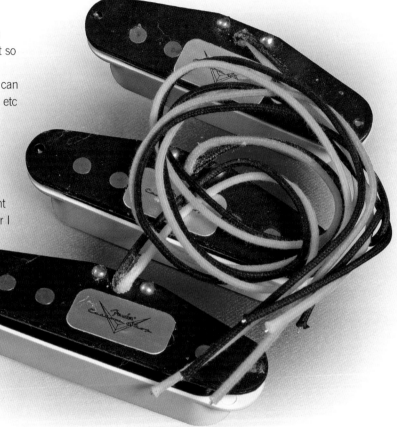

Fitting Texas Specials

1 Remove the strings. As usual, this should be done one string at a time and working in from the sixth and first to fifth and second etc, saving undue shock and strain on the neck. A string winder saves a lot of finger effort. Once the strings are all free of the machine heads, removing the 'curly ends' with a good set of wire cutters makes extraction through the bridge assembly a lot easier.

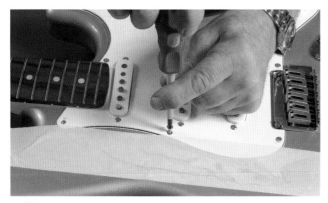

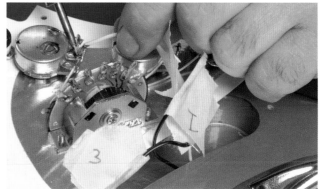

2 Unscrew the scratchplate with a Phillips '1' point screwdriver and stow the screws away safely in some sort of container.

Many modern Strats feature an extra fret, which means that care must be taken manoeuvring the scratchplate from under the lip that extends the fingerboard an extra quarter-inch or so to accommodate this additional fret.

3 Make a careful note of where your original pickup wires are connected – label the wires if necessary. Fender supply a clear diagram with the Texas Specials indicating the correct wiring arrangement, but it assumes you have a standard five-way Fender switch installed. However, you may not have this switch, so it is doubly important that you label all your wires before removal.

■ Following Leo Fender's original design concept, you can now remove the complete pickup and electrics assembly by simply unsoldering the jack socket, pickup selector connections, and tremolo earth/ground wires.

■ For this you will need a 25W soldering iron, an iron stand, and a wet sponge for removing redundant solder from the iron.

■ When removing the wires from the back of the control pots and pickup selector be as quick as possible, to avoid any heat damage to the pot.

4 Remove the trem ground wire at the pickup end as this will be easier – the trem end requires a bigger, hotter iron.

Having separated the pickup/scratchplate assembly put the neck body assembly in a safe place and continue.

■ Separate the pickup wiring loom with a sharp craft knife.

5 With a Phillips '1' point screwdriver, carefully remove the old pickups. Note the original equipment has metal springs to facilitate adjustment of the pickup heights. However, the Texas Specials and most top-of-the-range Strats feature soft latex washers in this role. John Diggins tells me this is probably because the latex affords better acoustic damping than springs. The snag, however, is that they naturally perish over time.

■ We will assume that you are going to use the supplied authentic latex option.

6 Carefully install the new pickups using the latex washers.

■ Note that the new pickups have authentic old-fashioned but wonderfully useful 'waxed' wire. Carefully remove all the modern cheap and nasty vinyl wire during your installation. An advantage of the old-fashioned stuff is that it's 'push back' wire, enabling you to ease the insulation back to expose the conductor for easy soldering.

■ Also note that the pickups are colour coded to identify their position – this is critical to the intended sound. Note particularly that the middle pickup is out of phase to aid a certain humbucking quality when the pickups are paired.

7 Mould the new wire into a neat loom and trim to the required length.

8 All three black common ground wires can be soldered together to the back of the volume pot. A wooden lollipop stick makes a good heat-insulated tool for holding the wires in place. The finished solder joint should be bright and shiny, indicating a good conducting medium – a 'dry ' joint will be dull, indicating a potential problem.

9 Solder the 'hot' wires (white) to the pickup selector according to your previous labelling.

NB: These connections are critical to retain the correct order of pickup selection.

10 Carefully tape your pickup looms with some masking tape.

11 Reassemble your completed pickup rig as originally found. This will entail restoring the trem ground/earth wire and the jack socket connections as per your labelled original connections. Usually the 'trims' of waxed cable are long enough to replace all of the remaining cheap vinyl wiring. Worth doing.

Pickup height settings

It is reasonable to assume that having the pickups set high and thereby closer to the strings will produce more output from your Strat and possibly more 'tone'. However, be aware that the magnetic field from conventional Strat pickups is strong enough to interfere with the natural excursion of the strings, which can result in very odd harmonic effects. Most notably the sixth string sounded at the 12th fret can produce odd 'beats' and very uneven intonation.

Fender have strict recommendations

1 Depress all of the strings at the last fret. Using a 6in (150mm) ruler, measure the distance from the bottom of the first and sixth strings to the top of the pole piece. As a rule of thumb, the distance should be greatest at the sixth string, for the neck pickup position, and closest at the first string, for the bridge pickup position.

Follow the measurement guidelines from the Fender chart below as a starting point. The distance will vary according to the amount of magnetic pull of your specific pickup.

In the last analysis you'll have to decide for yourself on the most effective compromise between output and magnetic interference.

Fender recommendations

	Bass side	Treble side
Texas Specials	%₄in (3.6mm)	%₄in (2.4mm)
Vintage style	%₄in (2.4mm)	%₄in (2mm)
Humbuckers	¼in (1.6mm)	%₄in (1.6mm)

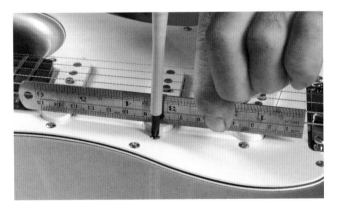

2 Using a Phillips '2' point screwdriver and an accurate metal ruler, adjust the height to the recommended starting point.

NB: Beware that when lowering the pickup extensively the pickup screw sometimes becomes disengaged from its socket. This procedure isn't recommended just before a gig, as relocating the screw usually means removing the pickguard!

84

Volume controls

Testing, cleaning and/or replacement of standard 250K pots.

■ So Why Would You Want To Do This?

The Strat's volume and tone controls are carbon based potentiometers, an invention of the late 19th and early 20th centuries. They are crude and mechanical but they work well. They do, however, generate 'dirt' by the nature of the mechanical friction of metal on carbon. This loose carbon inside the pot impedes the electrical contact and often causes it to be intermittent and prone to audible crackling. Corrosion of the metal parts adds 'snap' to the 'crackle'. We shall concentrate on the volume pots, as due to their more frequent use these are the ones most likely to fail.

■ A Little Background

Leo Fender left school in 1928, the year the first viable thermionic valves became commercially available. He was already an enthusiastic radio ham and was soon in business building and renting PA systems for local fairs. His formal start in business came in 1938, with Fender's Radio Service. He literally knocked on doors in the neighbourhood of his shop at the corner of Spadra and Santa Fe Boulevard, Fullerton, and offered to repair broken radios.

The simple tone and volume controls found in '30s radios – the 'resistive capacitor' circuits – are the basis for those still found in most Fender Stratocasters.

■ Understanding The Resistive Capacitor Circuit

If you alter the resistance of a circuit (in this case by turning your Strat's tone control) and that circuit also has a capacitor in circuit, which it does, the frequency response of that circuit will alter – we perceive this as a change in tone.

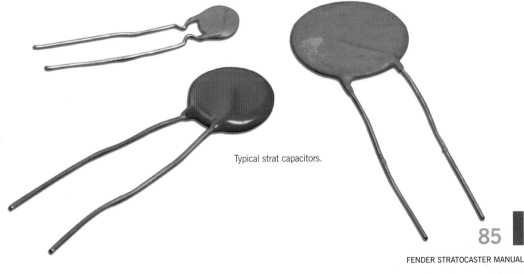

Typical strat capacitors.

Testing a pot to see if it is still functional

Tools required

- Phillips '1' point screwdriver
- Solder and 25W soldering iron
- An accurate electrical multimeter, with an option for ohms or resistance measurement

1 Remove the strings from the guitar and access the electrics by carefully removing the pickguard with a Phillips '1' point screwdriver. Keep the screws together in a small container.

2 Isolate the pot by first labelling then unsoldering the internal wiring. If you're slow with your soldering iron, then use a pair of crocodile clips or something similar as effective 'heat sinks' to draw heat away from other damageable components. John Diggins actually uses a set of surgical forceps that not only draw away heat, but have enough mass to hold things in position if required.

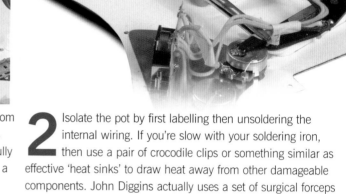

3 Set the multimeter to 'ohms' measurement in the 2M range. Zero the meter. Bring the multimeter probes into contact with the two outer connection prongs. A Vintage Strat volume or tone control should present a reading of 250K, give or take 20 per cent. A figure higher than this suggests the pot should be replaced.

NB: It's worth checking that the guitar has the correct pots fitted, as with an old guitar they may have been changed at some point. Sometimes the resistance value is marked on the pot casing.

- Some later Strats can have higher pot values, so it's important to check or on Fender's website for the appropriate values for your specific Strat model.

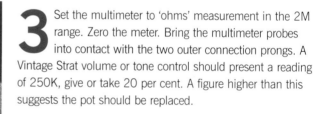

4 If the pot is giving the correct resistance value you can also test the smooth working of the carbon track.

- Apply one of the multimeter probes to one of the pot's outer prongs and the other to the middle prong. Use crocodile clips to hold the probes in position. The resistance value indicated on the multimeter should smoothly alter as you rotate the pot control. If the needle shows an intermittent response the pot may need cleaning.

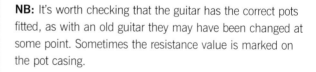

5 Repeat the process, this time testing the other outer prong in relation to the middle prong.

Cleaning

Sometimes a well-used pot can be restored to useful service by simple cleaning/lubrication. However, the replacement pots are so cheap and readily available nowadays it's worth considering replacement. Also, 'switch cleaner' works well on switches but less well on carbon pots.

1 If you have not already done so, slacken the guitar's strings enough to allow you to remove the pickguard.

NB: Modern Strats with the extra fret almost invariably require complete removal of the strings.

2 Using a Phillips '1' point screwdriver, unscrew the pickguard and keep the screws together in a small container.

3 Beware of the metal parts of the electrical assembly scratching the guitar finish as you carefully remove the pickguard. You may want to mask the finish with a lightly taped duster. The pickguard will not remove completely, as the pickup wiring is soldered to the output jack. However, you should have enough slack to access the pots.

The neck has been removed from this Strat for other work in progress.

4 Using the supplied hose, squirt a good quality switch or contact cleaner (eg Blue Shower or DeOxit) into the pot through the opening on the side of the case. If the pot is sealed, try cleaning via the microscopic gap around the shaft. You should try if possible to flush out any dirt. Also turn the pot shaft to allow the cleaning fluid to reach all of the contact points. Avoid getting switch cleaner on the guitar surface, and wear safety glasses to protect your eyes.

5 Carefully replace the pickguard assembly, retune the strings, and test the cleaned pot.

If You Still Have Noise Problems Or 'Dead Spots'

Everything mechanical eventually wears out, so consider a replacement pot. It makes a huge amount of sense to replace with an exact Fender-specification pot, readily available via the internet (see *Contacts* in appendix). The type 250K pots are available slightly cheaper from radio supply shops, but all pots are not created equal and you may find slight variances in shaft sizes etc which can cause problems.

Replacing a volume or tone control

NB: This will involve electrical soldering, so protect your eyes with safety glasses and cover any guitar parts that may be spattered by stray solder.

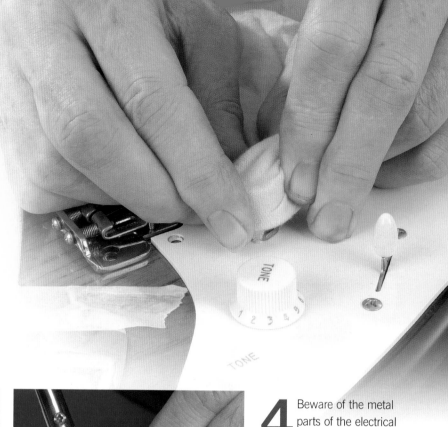

1 Remove the plastic knob from the offending control. These can become quite solidly fixed, so avoid damage to the guitar by using a soft rag wrapped around and under the knob for extra torque.

2 De-tension and if necessary remove the guitar strings (the preferred option).

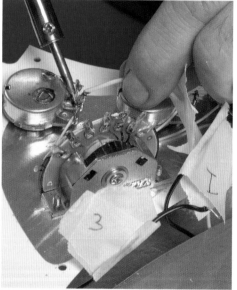

3 Using a Phillips '1' point screwdriver, unscrew the pickguard and keep the screws together in a small container.

4 Beware of the metal parts of the electrical assembly scratching the guitar finish as you carefully remove the pickguard. You may want to mask the finish with a lightly taped duster or some masking tape. The pickguard will not remove completely as the pickup wiring is soldered to the output jack. It is usually worth separating the pickup assembly completely by carefully unsoldering the output jack at the pickup end.

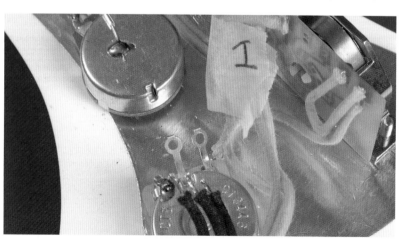

5 Label the cables connected to the old pot with some cloth-backed tape ('cloth backed' is easy to write on, though a sticky label wrapped back on itself works just as well), assign each cable a number, and draw yourself a little sketch of what goes where, noting the orientation of the tags on the old pot in relationship to the back of the pickguard. This sounds elementary but some old cables are not colour coded and there are alternative wiring options. Taking this approach restores your wiring intact and gets you back to the sound you've come to expect.

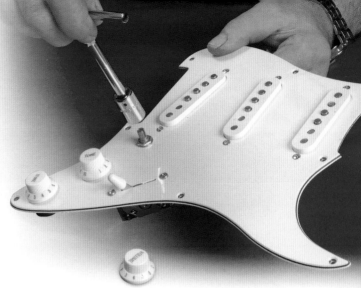

6 Place a crocodile clip or similar on the wiring between the pot and the pickups to act as a 'heat sink', absorbing heat that might otherwise find itself cooking your pickups. Carefully unsolder the old pot with the lowest rating soldering iron you have – 15W may work but a higher rated iron used quickly will be fine.

7 Use a socket-type spanner – the size will vary from model to model (see *Case Studies* on pages 106-146) – to unbolt the nut retaining the pot to the pickguard. (A socket-type spanner/wrench is less likely to mark the pickguard than a conventional spanner.)

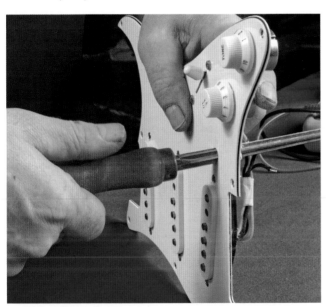

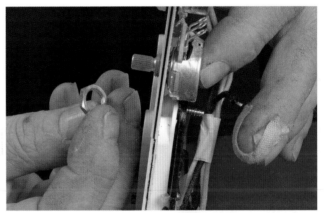

NB: Sometimes the new pot has a slightly larger shank, in which case you'll need to enlarge the pickguard hole with a rat tail file or similar.

8 Place the new pot in position, retaining the old orientation (refer to your diagram), and fix with the new retaining nut.

9 Tin the new connecting tags for the replacement pot with a little solder and solder them in place as per your labelling. A lollipop stick makes an effective aid and also doesn't waste any heat. Reassemble as before.

89

Nut adjustment

Classic Vintage Type Strat. A well set up nut can radically transform a guitar's performance.

A Word Of Warning

The Fender Stratocaster has one of the thinnest and most fragile nut types I've ever seen. The nut generally is also one of the most difficult and skilled adjustments/replacements for an amateur. Correct nut shaping – which is essential to ensure stable tuning, good tone and correct string spacing – is not a job to be taken lightly. Even if you're buying a pre-formed Strat nut you'll need specialist tools to make minor adjustments. If you're at all unsure of your skills or tooling then I recommend you take your Strat to a qualified guitar tech or luthier.

■ So why would you want to do this?

Wear in the nut slots, perhaps caused by the sawing action of extensive tremolo/vibrato use, can make the action at the nut/first fret too low, resulting in buzzing and snagging.

Another reason is to replace a cheap plastic nut with a bone substitute, which has better acoustic properties.

Replacing the nut

1 In order to remove the nut cleanly, first score any overlapping lacquer with a sharp scalpel, particularly on maple necks, which tend to be lacquered over the neck assembly. This scoring should ensure any chipping of the lacquer or polyester finish is controlled and confined.

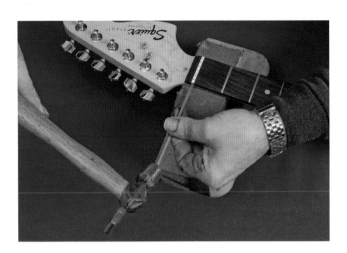

2 Remove the old nut. As you can see, the Vintage Stratocaster has a 'slot' type of nut housing, often as narrow as ⅛in inch. This rosewood board has no overlapping lacquer.

■ Tap the nut gently using a small hammer. With luck the nut should eventually become loose and can be removed as one piece reasonably easily.

■ As a last resort prise the nut out with a pair of smooth-ended pliers. The smooth ends will avoid damaging the old nut, which, assuming you were happy with your original string spacing, will provide a perfect template for the new spacing.

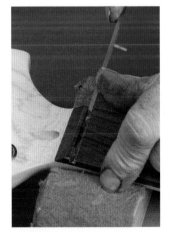

3 It is necessary to clean the nut slot of any surplus adhesive, lacquer, etc. A narrow and sharp chisel can be used as an effective scraper on both the end of the fingerboard and the bottom of the nut slot. A custom chisel slightly narrower than ⅛in is required.

4 Smooth the nut slot with a specialist 'nut seating file' specific to the Fender size (see *Contacts* in the appendix). It's important to avoid chipping the neck finish, so gently file the sharp edge of any lacquer and also file the nut bottom with inward strokes from both ends of the nut slot, thus avoiding accidentally pulling any lacquer from the neck.

5 Approximate the new nut blank. Begin with an oversize blank, which can then be shaped down to a custom fit.

NB: PLEASE use bone or synthetic Micarta, not endangered ivory!

7 Draw the fingerboard outline radius on to the new nut with a sharp pencil.

8 Add a pencil radius above the fingerboard outline. This new radius needs to be enough to account for the fret height, the string height, and the thickness of the string (a guitar tech might add a little more for good measure!). You will certainly need to allow a little more height towards the bass strings, as they need more room to vibrate without 'choking' on the first fret.

9 You can position the first two outer strings on the new nut by making pilot notches with a very fine craft saw (X-acto or similar, with a blade of .010 gauge or less).

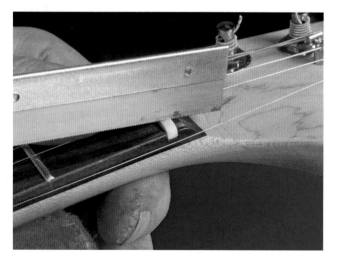

6 Measure your nut slot width and mark the required nut slots on your new blank based on the precise measurements of your nut slot and your old nut. Ideally you should carefully copy the string spacing from the old nut. Pay particular attention to the spacing of the sixth and first strings from the outside edge. Having strings too close to the edge will make finger vibrato difficult.

■ Check constantly for a snug and even fit in the nut slot. At this juncture the nut should still be left slightly overlong for flexibility at the later stages of shaping. A ⅛in edge overlap will be enough to allow for some fine tuning.

10 If for some reason you don't have the old nut then a specialist tool, a compensated nut spacing template (see *Contacts* in the appendix), is the easiest way to get even spacing between the outside of adjoining strings – a more important factor than equal spacing at their centres. Use this or the old nut to determine the position of the remaining string slots.

■ Surprising as it might seem, expert luthiers often determine the individual string spacing by eye. Though this sounds a little unscientific, the precise calculations in thousandths of an inch are made very complex by the fact that each string is a different gauge. (This is where the template can be used for reference.)

■ You can adopt the pro method to a degree by positioning the strings in very shallow 'pilot' slots, then making any minor adjustments by eye before completing actual filing of the final slots.

John prefers an X-acto
saw for most of this work.

Tech Tip

Graphite dust used for lock lubrication makes a good nut lubricant but it does tend to go everywhere when applied using the blower provided. Mixing a little graphite with some Vaseline petroleum jelly makes a useful and controllable lubricant paste. Apply it very sparingly.

John Diggins – Luthier

11 Carefully file the new slots to the depth marked on the new nut. Specialist precision nut files (see *Contacts* in appendix) will allow smoothing of the nut slot bottom without damaging the sides of the slot. These files have smooth edges and a round bottom and are available in the precise size for your chosen string gauges. In practice a luthier would use a slightly smaller file than the requisite slot and use a rolling technique on the forward motion to widen the slot with more control and less chance of the file snagging.

File at a back angle, as it is also necessary to shape the floor, or bottom, of the slot correctly, to enable the string to slide through it freely. If the slot isn't correctly shaped, it will prevent smooth tuning and will hamper the instrument's ability to return to tune, particularly after using the vibrato.

When a string binds in the nut slot, it makes a pinging sound as it breaks free of the slot. This ping is often attributed to the tremolo/vibrato, as it's the use of this device that triggers the release of the snagging. The nut will eventually need lubricating with graphite (*see page 64*).

The back angle of the slot will give good contact for the string, important for tone, while a first contact point at the front (fret end) of the nut will ensure correct intonation.

Ideally the bottom of the nut slot should be rounded as per the relevant string radius.

12 Secure the new nut in place with a couple of dabs of glue. Don't overdo the glue, as the nut may need removing again for correction.

13 Check the action at the 1st fret with the string depressed at the 3rd fret. A feeler gauge at 1st fret should register approximately .0035in.

Emergency measures

An alternative to a complete nut replacement, and useful in an emergency – especially if only one or two nut slots are too deep – is to recycle some material from the top of the nut (assuming excess is available) and use this as infilling material.

To do this, tape both sides of the nut with masking tape then take a coarse file and file the top of the nut approximately half the depth you expect to raise the slots. Catch the loose filings on a piece of paper.

Fill the offending slots with the loose filings. Then carefully soak the filings with thin superglue. Press the solution into place with a toothpick.

When dry, refile the slots, referring to the methods described above. As before, the slots should be made so that the string sits in about half to three-quarters of their diameter, though a Strat will cope quite well with a deep nut, especially if you're a 'heavy picker'. Slots should taper downwards on the tuner side, and again the strings' first point of contact must be at the fret side of the nut.

Pickup selection options and rewiring

Leo Fender liked the sound of solo single coil pickups. That's why the original Stratocaster was designed with a three-pole pickup selector, simply making one pickup available at a time. The thinking was built around the then current notion of 'lead' or 'treble' pickup for solos and two other pickups for different kinds of mellow accompaniment. Buddy Holly clearly thought along those lines for his solos and verses in his recording of the classic pop song *Peggy Sue*.

If you've ever found the middle Strat pickup slightly redundant you may want to consider the three-pickup design notion as 'one more' – in 1954 Gibson offered two-pickup guitars, so the revolutionary and competitive Fender company had three! One more – 30 years before Spinal Tap and their Marshall amplifier that 'went one more' – up to 11!

Very soon, however, creative guitarists discovered that crudely jamming Leo's three-way switch between positions with a matchstick created a whole new palette of interesting sounds. This creative improvisation made available the complex 'frequency dependent' phase combination and cancellation effects that so appeal to our ears.

These interesting sounds are the result of amplifying the sound of the same set of vibrating strings in two differing parts of their excursion at the same time. This random combination of two similar sounds with very slightly different time of arrival

and harmonic content is the basis of much that we enjoy in the sound of any instrument. Our ears love complexity, especially in phase relationships. This is also why we enjoy the sound of reverberation and echo whether real or artificially created. These 'FX' create very complex random phase relationships. What's happening when we combine pickups and/or add reverberation and delay is making the sound more complex, more intriguing, and our ears and brains love it.

Not for Leo Fender, however, who called the matchstick jamming effect 'the snarl'.

However, by 1965 the 'in-between' sounds had become an integral part of the Stratocaster sound and many players had modified their guitar switches or rewired the existing one to obtain these. Finally, in about 1977, Fender started to offer five-way switches as standard.

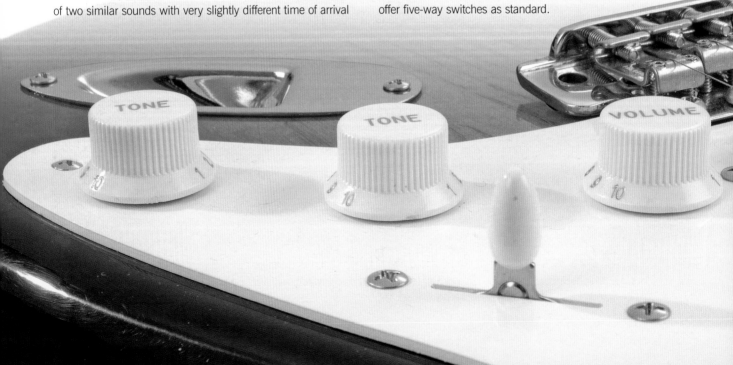

Fitting a five-way selector to a Vintage Strat

The replacement Fender five-way switch PN 017053 is readily available from www.fender.com and will fit into the existing pickguard slots without any modification. You may, however, want to consider the Schaller equivalent, which offers pickups one and three combined as well! (See *Contacts* in the appendix.)

Place the guitar on a protective surface. An old blanket on a sturdy table or workbench is ideal.

1 Remove the plastic control knob from the existing selector switch. This is a push fit and should come away easily.

2 Remove the guitar strings, one at a time and working towards the middle – ie take the sixth and first strings off, then second and fifth, etc, so that the strain loss on the neck is even and gradual. Though many experienced guitar techs remove all the strings at once with a set of wire cutters, they can solve all the problems this potentially causes relatively quickly, whereas you probably don't have that skill and experience. I therefore recommend the slower and more stable approach. The less sudden the change you impose on an instrument the more stable it is and the less need for a guitar tech. If you have a guitar tech then you don't need this book!

3 Carefully remove the pickguard screws with a Phillips '1' point screwdriver. Store the screws in a small container for safety.

4 Carefully remove the pickguard, ensuring you don't put undue strain on the electrical loom and that you avoid causing any damage as you ease the guard from under the extended fingerboard.

FIGURE 1

Neck tone control

To lug 2

T

Ground to volume pot

To lug 1

T

Middle tone control

Also see photo on page 96

5 If you find the diagram above easy to follow, fine. If not, label your existing wires 1, 2, 3, 4, 5, and 6 and draw yourself a custom diagram that you can comfortably follow.

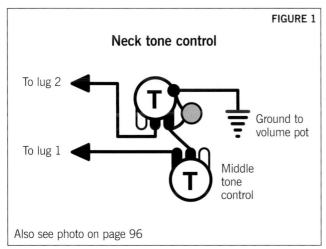

6 Carefully unsolder the old three-pole switch.

7 Protecting the guitar finish with a carefully placed duster or masking tape, slowly unscrew the old switch mounting screws using a '1' or '2' point Phillips screwdriver (depending on the model). Rushing this process will inevitably damage some of the screw edge and eventually make the screws difficult to remove. Taking out the screws slowly and firmly will avoid slippage and you're less likely to scratch the pickguard. Note the position of the old switch – which side is the fibre insulation?

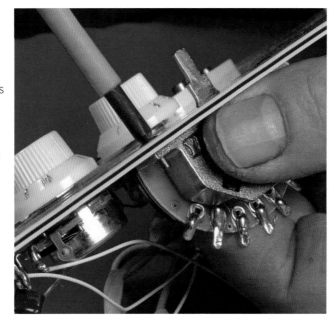

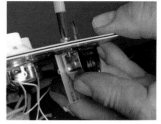

8 Place the new switch in position, taking care to ensure it's the same way up as your original – which side is the insulation? Screw the switch in place using the existing screws.

9 Tin the new switch connections with a minimum of solder.

10 Carefully resolder the existing wires following the switch diagram in Figure 1 or your custom diagram. Use a minimum of solder and contact the components with the iron for just long enough to heat the solder. There are options on the pickup selections available and the tone control allocation. These depend on the make and model of the replacement switch, so follow the suppliers' guidelines.

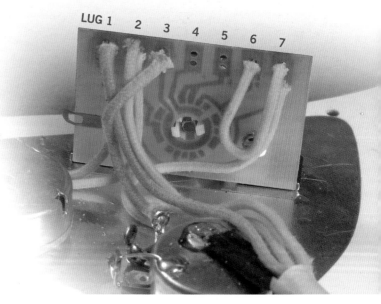

LUG 1   2   3   4   5   6   7

🖊 Tech Tip

When removing any plastic panels on a Stratocaster take care not to overtighten the chrome screws on reassembly – the plastic is easily cracked.

John Diggins – Luthier

11 Replace the pickguard in position and carefully screw it down.

12 Restring the guitar, first and sixth string first, etc, as before, and gradually ease up to full tension. With luck the guitar neck will go back to its former position. If not, refer to the set up and tuning section of the manual.

13

Test the new switching. A tuning fork held over the pickups easily indicates which pickups are on in which selector position. You should get:

Position 1: Bridge pickup only.
Position 2: Bridge and middle.
Position 3: Middle only. (NB: The Schaller E Model Mega switch option gives neck and bridge.)
Position 4: Middle and neck.
Position 5: Neck only.

For the solo sound on Eric Clapton's 'Wonderful Tonight' try position 4 combined with 20 years of practice!

Latest switching options

The Stratocaster continues to evolve, and in 2006 the latest innovation is a novel switch built into the volume control knob. This option, available on a number of American Strats, gives a greater variety of pickup combinations and thus offers a wider range of sounds.

Currently the single coil switching options are shown below.

5 Way SW Positions – S–1 Switch Up					
					Position
MV T1	MV T1+T2	MV T2	MV T2	MV T2	Controls
⬛	⬛	⬜	⬜	⬜	Neck (A)
⬜	⬛	⬛	⬛	⬜	Middle (B)
⬜	⬜	⬜	⬛	⬛	Bridge (C)
	A/B		B/C		Connection

5 Way SW Positions – S–1 Switch Down					
					Position
MV T1	MV T1+T2	MV T2	MV T2	MV T2	Controls
⬛	⬛	⬛	⬜	⬜	Neck (A)
⬛	⬛	⬛	⬛	⬛	Middle (B)
⬜	⬜	⬛	⬛	⬛	Bridge (C)
A+B	(A/SC) + B	(A/C) + B	B + (C/SC)	B+C	Connection

SC – Special Capacitor
T1 – Neck Tone Control

T2 – Mid/Bridge Tone Control
/ – Parallel Connection

+ – Series Connection
MV – Master Volume

⬛ – Pickup ON
⬜ – Pickup OFF

Truss rod adjustment

The Vintage Strat truss rod adjusts at the heel of the neck, which is difficult to access. This Standard truss rod can counteract concave curvature, for example in a neck that has too much relief, by generating a force in the neck opposite to that caused by excessive string tension.

⚡ Tech Tip

You *can* loosen the strings a little and then undo the two back neck screws. This then enables you to tip the neck up enough to reach the rod screw. But I don't usually do this in front of the client – it looks horrendous!

Andy Gibson – Luthier

'Vintage' adjustment

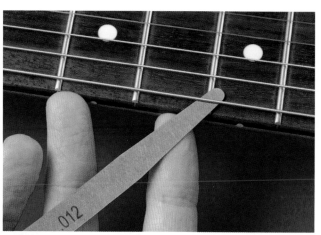

1 Check your tuning (which should be at standard A440 pitch or your preferred and consistent 'custom pitch').

Next we need to check the neck for relief – is it straight, or bowed either convex or concave?

Install a capo at the 1st fret, depress the sixth string at the last fret.

2 With a feeler gauge, check the gap between the bottom of the string and the top of the 8th fret. See the specification chart overpage for the correct gap. This will vary depending on the radius of your particular neck type.

If the neck is too concave (indicated by too big a gap measured with the feeler gauge) then you may consider adjusting the truss rod.

Do NOT do this on a rare and precious guitar if you feel unqualified. Talk instead to an experienced guitar tech via your local music shop.

3 Slacken the strings. Then, using a '2' point Phillips screwdriver carefully unscrew the four neck bolts approximately ⅛in at the top and 1in at the back – this should be enough to tilt the neck back for access to the truss rod screw.

NB: If present, be very careful to note the position of any neck shims (small slivers of wood or card in the neck pocket), as they must remain in the same position when the neck is reseated.

Access to the truss rod on Vintage and Reissue '50s and '60s Strats varies, as some have a small cut-out indentation in the pickguard to enable easier access. Generally the earliest guitars and their reissues do not have this. With these guitars you may have to unscrew the neck bolts slightly more to access the truss rod and avoid the risk of damaging the pickguard.

4 Adjust the truss rod screw a quarter-turn clockwise.

NB: Although this is really a job for a straight head 8mm or ¹¹⁄₃₂in screwdriver, with the difficult access involved a '2' point Phillips often works well and risks less damage to the plastic pickguard.

5 Alternatively, if the neck is too convex (strings too close to the fingerboard), turn the truss rod nut a quarter turn anti-clockwise to allow the string tension to pull more relief into the neck.

NB: For obvious reasons the Vintage truss rod was originally conceived to adjust situations with too much relief – it is much more likely to be successful in this application.

6 Checking that any shims are correctly reseated, replace the neck and re-tension the strings to correct pitch.

7 Recheck the relief gap with the feeler gauge and readjust as required.

NB: In either case, if you meet excessive resistance when adjusting the truss rod, or your instrument needs constant adjustment, or adjusting the truss rod has no effect on the neck, take your instrument to a local musical instrument shop and seek advice.

Fender recommended neck relief

Neck radius	Relief
7.25in	.012in (0.3mm)
9.5in to 12in	.010in (0.25mm)
15in to 17in	.008in (0.2mm)

NB: You may need to reset the individual string height following truss rod adjustment – see the chapter on *Setting up and tuning.*

Later Strats
Later Strats have three different kinds of truss rod, including the 'Bi-flex' variety.

There are two types of Standard truss rod: one that adjusts at the heel of the neck, and another which adjusts at the headstock. For heel type truss rods see previous text.

The Standard truss rod can counteract concave curvature, for example in a neck that has too much relief, by generating a force in the neck opposite to that caused by excessive string tension. Fender became aware of the issue of convex necks as players switched to lighter gauge strings.

The 'Bi-Flex' truss rod system
The Bi-Flex Truss Rod (used on most American and American Deluxe Series instruments) was introduced by Fender in the early '80s. Unlike the Standard truss rods, which can only correct a neck that is too concave (under-bowed), the Bi-Flex can compensate for either concave (under-bowed) or convex (over-bowed) curvature, by generating a force in either direction as needed.

Tightened as usual the truss rod nut bows the neck backwards. As you loosen the nut you'll find the neck's neutral. If you continue to loosen the nut you'll feel a renewed tightening as the rod pushes against a walnut dowel, causing the neck to bow forward.

Headstock truss rod access

1 Check your tuning (which should be at standard A440 pitch or your preferred and consistent 'custom pitch').

Install a capo at the 1st fret, depress the sixth string at the last fret.

2 With a feeler gauge, check the gap between the bottom of the string and the top of the 8th fret. See the specification chart on the previous page for the correct gap. This will vary depending on the radius of your particular neck type.

If the neck is too concave (indicated by too big a gap measured with the feeler gauge) then you may consider adjusting the truss rod. Do NOT do this if you feel unqualified.

Optional check without strings

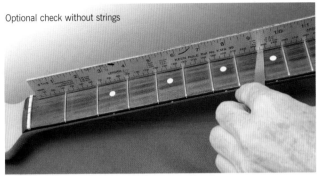

3 Adjustment at headstock. (NB: Allen key sizes vary depending on the model and date: refer to the case studies *page 102* for guidance.)

First sight down the edge of the fingerboard from behind the headstock, looking toward the body of the instrument. **NB:** A flat neck without string tension is a good start, so many techs make this adjustment without strings. A 'straight edge' tool makes the job simpler.

4 Turn the truss rod nut clockwise to remove excess relief. If the neck is too convex (strings too close to the fingerboard), turn the truss rod nut counter-clockwise to allow the string tension to pull more relief into the neck.

5 Restring and check your tuning, then recheck the gap with the feeler gauge and readjust as necessary.

NB: If you meet excessive resistance when adjusting the truss rod, or your instrument seems to need constant adjustment, or adjusting the truss rod has no effect on the neck, then take the instrument to a qualified guitar tech.

Shimming and micro-tilt adjustment

Another factor to consider with neck alignment is the precise pitch of the neck in relation to the body. Shimming is a procedure used to adjust the pitch of the neck.

On many of the American Series guitars, a Micro-Tilt adjustment is offered. This uses an Allen key working against a plate installed in the butt-end of the neck. The need to adjust the pitch (raising the butt-end of the neck in the pocket, thereby pitching the neck back) of the neck occurs in situations where the string height is high and the action adjustment is as low as the bridge adjustment will allow.

For those guitars with the Micro-Tilt adjustment, loosen the two neck screws on both sides of the adjustment access hole on the neckplate by at least four full turns. Tightening the hex adjustment screw with a ⅛in hex wrench by

approximately a quarter-turn will allow you to raise the action approximately ¹⁄₃₂in. Retighten the neck screws when the adjustment is complete.

Specific case studies

In its 50-plus year history there have been over 100 variants to the Stratocaster marque. However, most of Leo Fender's essential elements remain. It is clearly not within the scope of this book to cover all 100 variants. However, the following case studies cover many of the principal points.

LEFT The case study guitars.

RIGHT A Mexican made 'Fat Strat'.

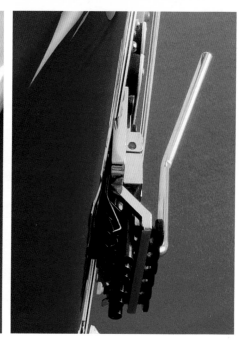

Case study variants

Country of manufacture is a major factor and I have covered four USA Strats plus Japanese, Indonesian, Chinese, and Mexican guitars.

Screw sizes have remained fairly consistent throughout the Strat's history, though nut, bolt, and Allen key sizes vary across the Imperial and metric divide. I have given specific guidance throughout.

In the course of my research I have identified several distinct Strat groupings:

■ Late prototypes

The 1954–6 Stratocaster and reissues mark a beginning for this radical guitar. I'm sure Leo didn't yet see it as finished, indeed he talked generically of a constantly evolving 'Fender Guitar'. Certainly the clubby neck shape that harked back to the early lack of a truss rod was open to evolution, especially as the metal truss rod proved a success, enabling the bulk wood of the neck to be pared down. Also the '50s were early days for plastics and Leo seemed to be constantly searching for successful plastic formulae and moulding methods. The early rounded pickup covers were not a success, being prone to transparency and cracking. Similiarly the volume and tone knobs needed to evolve a more futuristic, less Radio Shack appearance. Custom colours were very rare at this stage – guitars were still predominantly the colour of wood. An integral fingerboard still seemed a good idea.

◼ 1957
An evolved, streamlined guitar with a neck still very much emulated today. Custom colours were proving surprisingly popular. Cloth covered internal wiring.

◼ 1959-65
Triple-ply fingerboards were less prone to warping and clearly some players were wearing out the original maple necks, leaving Leo to consider the benefits of a removable and very hard rosewood fingerboard.

◼ 1965-85
The CBS years – corporate rationalisation and loss of ground roots musician input.

◼ 1985
The management buyout and the rebirth of a legend. The search for a new Standard Stratocaster.

◼ 1985 to the present day
The proliferation of variants: Beginners' Stratocasters, Heavy Metal Stratocasters, Artist Series guitars, and the evolution of the Custom Shop.

◼ All these variants are to some extent covered here and the core elements of your guitar should be reflected in the following case studies, at least in principle.

USA-made '54 Custom Shop

This particular example is '5075' of a limited edition of 1,954 guitars (presumably meaning it is number 75). Made in 2004, it's a handmade instrument signed by Custom Shop master craftsman John Cruz. In every tiny detail it closely resembles what Leo and George may have made one week in 1954.

General description

Superficially this may look like any other Stratocaster. However, a closer look reveals a fantastic attention to authentic 1954 detail.

■ The volume and tone knobs have a 'wireless radio' shape, less 'stratospheric' than the ones that emerged in the later '50s. The three-way switch knob is also more '50s in shape.

■ The pickup covers are rounded at the edges – again more early than late 20th century. I'm reliably told that all these components are made not of Bakelite but of ABS Acrylonitrile Butadiene Styrene, and were injection moulded for the most part, except for the pickguard, which was cut from yet another plastic formula. Available since the 1940s, Styrene Acrylonitrile copolymers were initially fragile, and this limitation led to the introduction of a rubber (butadiene) as a third monomer. This revised formulation first became available in the 1950s, so the Stratocaster was very much a child of its time.

■ The fingerboard is also single ply white plastic with eight Phillips number '1' size screws. The tremolo arm has a vintage type 5/32in thread on a 3/16in shank and is angled very high by modern standards.

■ The body contours are the original generous vintage 'deep' type. Bill Carson would have loved it. The wood is a beautifully open grained ash with a two-colour sunburst nitrocellulose lacquer. Leo switched from ash to alder during the first two years of manufacture due to the tendency for there to be a raised grain in the ash that was then available. This has been observed in several '54 guitars.

■ Bridge

Underneath the 'ashtray', which like all the chrome parts has an aged vintage look, are six pressed steel saddles with the early 'Patent pending' stamp. The 'ashtray' truly looks like it belongs rather than having simply been added as an afterthought trim. The saddles require the expected 0.05in Allen for height adjustment and are custom filed to avoid removing the flesh on the heel of your hand – a nice touch. The string length adjustment requires the usual Vintage '1' point Phillips head.

It was interesting to play the '54 with the chromed saddle cover 'ashtray' in place. On this particular guitar it significantly affected the sound. A curious resonance is created by the enclosed cavity and the synergy of the linked saddles. Playing a Buddy Holly riff with a touch of spring reverb on an old tube amplifier opens up a whole new world of 'early music' on authentic instruments. I cannot replicate this effect on the reissue '57!*

*Though Buddy Holly did play a guitar of this type it was stolen, and his last instrument was in fact a '58, serial number 028228, with a three-tone Sunburst finish and C profile neck not dissimilar to the '57 Reissue examined below.

■ Body

The body is a comfortable 8lb, slightly lighter than the usual Vintage Reissue. The body thickness is approximately 1.75in, though it seems thinner due to the very deep body contours.

■ Neck

The neck profile follows a typical 1954 'U' shape, chunky at the headstock end and thinner at the 'dusty end' of the fingerboard.

■ The truss rod access is at the heel end, requiring a 5/16in straight blade screwdriver, the 'star' configuration being two straight blade options. See the Appendix for more on Strat neck profiles. The frets are .086in gauge and beautifully dressed and polished.

■ The neck is a nice piece of authentic nitrocellulose-coated maple with the frets set straight into the timber. The authentic dot markers have the appearance of black Bakelite. The ageing on the neck is subtle and convincing, and the 'skunk stripe' is tastefully colour-matched to the sunburst. The neck radius is a classic 7.25in and this is matched perfectly at the saddles.

■ The nut is a well cut piece of yellowing bone.

■ The machine heads are aged Fender/Klusons by Gotoh, but so far without any gear teeth missing. These work just fine, if a little 'Vintage stiff'.

■ There is one improvised string tree for the first and second strings made of an old round rivet ferule with a '1' point Phillips screw attaching it to the headstock.

■ The trem/vibrato is naturally of the Vintage type. Removing the rear plastic trem cover reveals three springs arranged in parallel, and a very substantial solid cast trem block with no taper. The trem claw requires the standard '2' point Phillips screwdriver.

■ The trem access cover has 'period feature' round string holes and a serial number.

■ It's a small point, but John Cruz has placed the top horn strap button in an unusual position – I guess he has seen it here on an original vintage '54.

Specific routine maintenance

First check the neck relief with your feeler gauges. The neck should be fairly flat – perhaps .015 relief at the 7th fret given .012in at the first fret. If the neck relief does need adjustment the '54 requires a ⅜in straight blade screwdriver at the heel.

Follow the Vintage Strat set up guide on *pages 32-37* for any saddle height and intonation adjustment.

The strings – which on this guitar are authentically NOT Fender bullets – are '10's with a plain third, as opposed to authentic '50s 'tow ropes'. The guitar is very much set up for modern strings and modern playing styles.

When changing strings, it's worth checking the machine-head fixing screws, which tend to work loose. On the '54 this requires a '1' point Phillips. Do not over-tighten them – just enough to stop the machine head moving in normal use.

At the same time check the string tree – the '1' point Phillips screw also tends to vibrate loose. This can affect tuning stability especially when using the trem/vibrato. Lubricating the underneath of the round ferule with a little ChapStick will prevent any sticking.

Whilst you have the tools out it's worth tightening the output jack retainer. This also tends to work loose, causing crackles and intermittent output. Tightening entails removing the recessed jack socket using a '1' point Phillips and getting a grip on the jack retainer itself as you tighten the bolt with a 0.5in socket spanner.

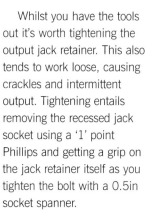

Under the hood

Removing the pickguard using the usual '1' point Phillips screwdriver reveals a beautifully clean rout, signed and carved with his initials by John Cruz. The minimum of wood has been removed, returning to the original Fender concept of 'a railway sleeper with strings'. It's interesting to compare this rout with that of a current American Series guitar.

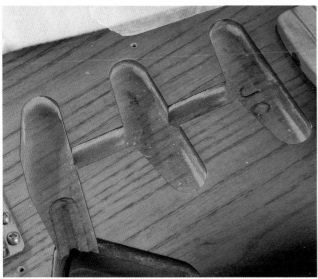

■ The wiring is impeccable, with three classic 250K pots and a 0.1mF capacitor routed via an interesting spring-loaded three-way switch. All the wire seems to be 'period authentic' wax-coated cloth, and I have never seen a neater cable loom.

■ The only electrical screening is a thick metal plate confined to the area above the potentiometers.

■ The heavily wound pickups in their '54 rounded cases have rubber washers instead of the later springs for fixing their height from the fingerboard.

■ If loose, the volume and tone pots require a 0.5in socket spanner for removal or adjustment.

NB: A stiff plastic knob can often be removed without damage by the careful use of a duster as an anchor. Never lever these plastic knobs with a screwdriver!

Signed off

I wouldn't presume to improve on John Cruz's impeccable set up of this classic and rather beautiful instrument. He has constructed a worthy tribute to an iconic piece of popular music history – I'm sure Leo Fender would have loved it.

For more pictures of the '54 see page 18

USA-made '57 Vintage Reissue

Serial No. V041930.

Made in 1996, this guitar represents a typical example of the current Fender reissues of their 'golden age' Stratocasters. It has been built to closely resemble a guitar produced in 1957 and originally had an 'as new' finish and came supplied in an authentic late '50s plush-lined case.

General description

Superficially this may look like any other Stratocaster. However, a closer look reveals some attention to authentic 1957 detail.

■ The volume and tone knobs are the late '50s type still employed in 2006.

■ The five-way switch is an alternative offered with this model, though the three-way switch would have still been standard in '57.

■ The pickup covers are sharp at the edges, again following the pattern adopted in 1955–6.

■ The fingerboard is single-ply white plastic with eight Phillips '1' slot size screws.

■ The tremolo arm has a Vintage-type 10-32 UNF thread on a ³⁄₁₆in shank and has the current moderate angle.

■ The body contours are the original generous Vintage 'deep' type, though not as pronounced as the '54 Reissue, especially on the rear scoop. The wood is alder with a coating of Fiesta Red in nitrocellulose lacquer with a polyurethane undercoat.

■ Bridge

Underneath the 'ashtray', which like all the chrome parts has an aged vintage look, are six pressed steel saddles with the 'Fender' stamp. The saddles require the expected .05in Allen for height adjustment. The string length adjustment requires the usual Vintage '1' point Phillips head.

■ Body

A comfortable 8.25lb, slightly heavier than the '54 Reissue. The body thickness is approximately 1.75in.

■ Neck

Follows a typical 1957 thinline 'C' profile with a constant taper to the body.

The neck is a nice piece of maple with the frets set straight into the timber. The authentic dot markers are black.

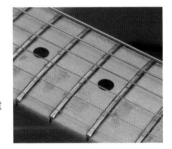

■ The truss rod access is at the heel end, requiring a ⁵⁄₁₆in straight blade screwdriver, the 'star' configuration being two straight blade options. See the appendix for more on Strat neck profiles. The frets are .086in gauge and show some slight wear.

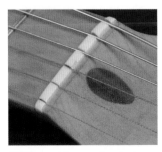

■ The nut is a well cut piece of bone-like plastic that Fender call Cyclovac, a very dense plastic imitation bone.

■ The machine heads are ageing Fender/Klusons by Gotoh, but so far without any gear teeth missing.

Condition on arrival

The guitar has been well played in over the last nine years and this shows on the maple neck, which exhibits considerable flaking of the polyurethane finish. Strictly speaking, for a '50s-type guitar this finish should be nitrocellulose, but due to environmental issues the general factory use of this substance is now strictly limited by California law.

Luthier John Diggins feels the original finish would be harder wearing and proposes that the guitar be repaired blending the new nitrocellulose with the factory polyurethane. The body also has one or two minor dings, for which John proposes an invisible repair.

For more detail on paintwork repairs *see page 70.*

■ The 'skunk stripe' is lighter than that of the '54. The neck radius is a classic 7.25in and this is matched perfectly at the saddles except for the low E, which is set slightly higher.

■ By 1957 the rear string access holes had changed to a more generous oval. Note the crack due to an over-tightened fixing screw.

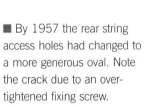

■ The trem/vibrato is of the Vintage type, and has three springs arranged in a trapeze, with a big solid cast trem block with no taper. The trem claw requires the standard '2' point Phillips screwdriver.

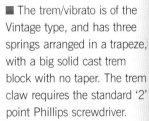

■ The top horn strap button is now in the accepted location.

■ There is one string tree of the seagull-wing type with a '0' point Phillips screw attaching it to the headstock.

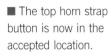

Specific routine maintenance

First check the neck relief with your feeler gauges. The neck should be fairly flat – perhaps .015 relief at the 7th fret. If the neck does need adjustment the '57 requires a ⁵⁄₁₆in straight blade screwdriver at the heel.

Follow the Vintage Strat set up guide (*page 32-36*) for any saddle and intonation adjustments.

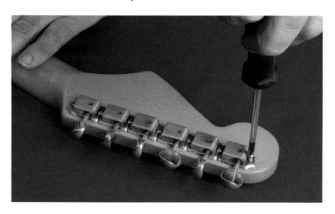

The strings on this guitar are .009 D'Addarios. When changing strings, it's worth checking the machine-head fixing screws, which tend to work loose. On the '57 this requires a '1' point Phillips. Do not over-tighten them – just enough to stop the machine head moving in normal use.

At the same time check the string tree – the '0' point Phillips screw also tends to vibrate loose. This can affect tuning stability, especially when using the trem/vibrato. Lubricating the underneath of the seagull with a little ChapStick will prevent any sticking.

Whilst you have the tools out it's worth tightening the output jack retainer. This tends to work loose, causing crackles and intermittent output. Tightening entails removing the recessed jack socket using a '1' point Phillips and getting a grip on the jack retainer itself as you tighten the bolt with a 0.5in socket spanner.

'Under the hood'

Removing the pickguard using the usual '1' point Phillips screwdriver reveals a beautifully clean rout. The minimum of wood has been removed, returning to the original Fender concept of 'a railway sleeper with strings'. Remember the other use for the Fender 'ashtray' – for retaining loose screws. An aerosol lid does just as well.

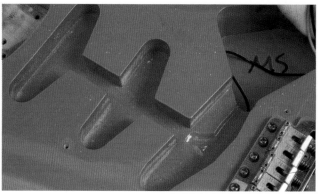

■ The wiring is impeccable, with three classic 250K pots and .1mF capacitors routed via a modern five-way switch. All the wire seems to be a wax-coated cloth.

■ The heavily wound pickups in their '57 cases still have rubber washers for fixing their height from the fingerboard, instead of the springs used in 'economy' Strats.

■ The only electrical screening is a thin metal plate confined to the area above the potentiometers.

■ If loose, the volume and tone pots require a 0.5in socket spanner for removal or adjustment.

Signed off

Following the neck refinish and the paintwork touch-up the '57 Reissue looks better than it did when I purchased it in '98.

Also, the nitrocellulose finish on the neck looks better and I'm told will be more hard-wearing. *See page 70*

The neck work had to be done, as this is a working instrument and the maple was beginning to shred at the points where the polyurethane finish was worn through. Also the bodywork dings look better having been filled and repainted. The neck socket area paint was flaking badly, largely due, I'm told, to the use of a polyurethane undercoat. Hopefully John's repair will halt the flaking for some time.

I have to say I wouldn't advocate this sort of cosmetic bodywork repair on a genuine rare 1950s instrument, but on a repro like this it seems less drastic. At least it demonstrates that minor paintwork repairs can be tastefully done if you have the necessary skills and equipment.

Chinese-made Squier

A Squier Affinity series Strat made in China in the 1990s. An excellent budget guitar clearly aimed at young students, an application in which its light weight and economic price will be well recieved. For teaching situations this guitar looks like and sounds like a Stratocaster.

Serial No. CY 010834.

General description

Superficially this Chinese Strat bears an 'Affinity' to the 1959 Vintage Stratocaster. To the casual viewer there is little of significant visual difference. The pickguard is single-ply plastic with eight Phillips '1' slot-size screws. Even the tremolo arm takes a Vintage-type thread of 10-32 UNF on a ³⁄₁₆in shank.

The body contours are of the generous Vintage 'deep' type. This stems from Leo's original consultations with Bill Carson and other early Fender players, who often complained the Telecaster slab body could dig into your ribs.

However

■ The body is significantly lighter, overall guitar weight about 7lb compared with a typical 8.25lb for a Vintage Reissue. The body is also thinner, approximately 1.5in compared with the classic 1.75in. The guitar is probably made of a South-East Asian conifer wood known as Agathis, though the heavy coat of polyurethane makes this impossible to determine definitively.

■ The neck profile follows a comfortable 1959 pattern. The headstock has a late '60s/early '70s vibe – large and with a recessed truss rod access.

■ The machine heads are of the modern bolt-on Fender/Gotoh type. There are two string trees for the first to fourth strings, of the seagull-wing type.

■ The trem/vibrato is also of the Vintage type, with three springs, but also has two significant differences that may affect the guitar's sound: the body routing is more extensive and deeper than a Vintage Reissue – significantly more wood has been removed – and the trem block has substantially less mass, being thinner and made from a light alloy.

■ Unlike a 1957, the fingerboard is a slab of dark hardwood with a rosewood-like grain and has 'mother of plastic' dot markers. The nut is also 'mother of plastic'.

■ There is no need for a 'skunk stripe' as the truss rod has been inserted before the fingerboard. The fingerboard has a modern American Series radius of 9.5in.

Condition on arrival

This good little runner has done a couple of years' service for the local educational 'Music Service'. It was in a sorry state with an action like Robin Hood's best longbow and a trem locked to the floor. It arrived missing a few parts, including a trem arm and the five-way selector knob.

Tech Tip

If the frets seem a little unfinished – which is normal on an economy guitar – take the opportunity to polish the frets with some very fine '40' grade wire wool. To do this either mask the fretboard with tape or use a proprietary metal fret guard.

Andy Gibson – Luthier

Specific routine maintenance

When you're next changing, strings it's worth checking the machine-head locking nuts, which tend to work loose. On the Chinese Squier this requires a 10mm socket spanner. Do not over-tighten them – just enough to stop the machine head moving in normal use.

At the same time check the string trees – the 'O' point Phillips screws also tend to work loose. This can affect tuning

Setting the string heights

The Affinity has a Vintage-type bridge arrangement but with cast saddles as opposed to the classic pressed steel.

The Allen key adjustment requires a 1.54mm key. Otherwise follow the instructions given for the Vintage Strat on *page 30*.

stability, especially when using the trem/vibrato. Lubricating the tree grooves with a little ChapStick prevents any sticking. This may be easier done by removing the tree and applying some ChapStick/Vaseline with a cocktail stick.

This guitar was supplied with Fender 'Bullet' strings – these guarantee a cosy fit for the strings in the trem block, which may help tuning stability. However, the fit can sometimes be too cosy.

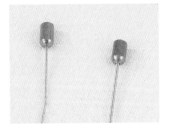

The rosewood-type fingerboard tends to dry out and will benefit from a little lemon oil – see *Contacts* in the appendix.

Whilst you have the tools out it's worth tightening the output jack retainer. This tends to work loose causing crackles and intermittent output. Tightening sometimes entails removing the recessed jack socket using a '1' point Phillips and getting a grip on the jack retainer itself as you tighten the bolt with a 12mm socket spanner. See *Know your Vintage Strat* on pages 19-23 for more on this plus photos.

'Under the hood'

As you might expect with a budget guitar, removing the pickguard using a '1' point Phillips screwdriver reveals a large double cavity but not quite a 'swimming pool'. In fact the guitar is so thin that the claw retainer screws have protruded into this front cavity. No harm done, but a little untidy. These large cavities will have some impact on the sound of the guitar.

■ The pickups are budget types with the effective magnetic pull coming not from the pole pieces themselves, which are quite weak, but from a common bar magnet which sits across the back of these. The sound, however, is surprisingly very good. There is no mistaking the familiar Strat snap, and interestingly the measured output from the crude magnets is equal to that from my Vintage '57.

Signed off

The Affinity responded well to a minimum of attention. The truss rod had almost no tension as found, explaining the bowed neck – a couple of turns resulted in a flattish neck with the recommended relief. *See page 25, 'Know your American Series Strat'*, for adjustment details.

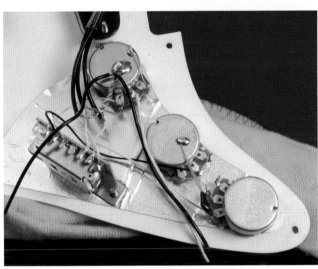

■ If loose, the volume and tone pots require a ⁷⁄₁₆in socket spanner (wrench) for removal or adjustment. The tone pots are a 500K type more common on humbucker guitars than Strats, and these and the five-way selector have a minimal screening foil attached to the pickguard rear. A 473K (.47mF) 100V capacitor sits across the two tone controls.

■ The five-pole switch is of a PCB type common on budget guitars. This would not be ideal for extensive professional use, but is adequate on what is intended as a student guitar.

The saddles were originally set too high with a random radius. This responded to the set-up as per the Vintage Strat *see page 30*.

The trem needed balancing but again responded easily to a typical Vintage set-up.

The pickup height setting is held in place effectively, if a little crudely, by a couple of springs.

Overall the guitar does feel a little crude and slightly unfinished. The tremolo/vibrato particularly, despite a set-up, seems unresponsive and 'dull' – probably due to the much lower mass in the trem block. However, with a new set of strings the guitar plays almost as well as my Corona made '57 Reissue! This is remarkable for a budget instrument and great testament to Leo Fender's original workmanlike plan.

This guitar provided the test bed for a number of upgrades described in this book. See 'Replacing the nut' *page 90*, 'Improving screening and reducing radio frequency induction' *page 66*.

Mexican-made 'Fat Strat'

Fenders answer to the trend for 'Superstrats' is to offer their own humbucker equipped guitars. These also offer the option of a Floyd Rose 'Super Trem'.

Serial No. MN 9 405385.

General description

This Midnight Blue Strat has perhaps been built with an eye on the early 21st-century Spinal Tap Tribute Band market. The locking trem is clearly designed for enthusiastic divebombing and the Fender humbucker is a nod in the direction of the number 11 dot on the volume dial. I'm sure it will do the job just fine after a little setting up.

■ The tremolo/vibrato assembly built by Floyd Rose is a Mark 11 model, having individual fine tuners and heavy duty saddles. For more on this see the specific set-up guide below.

■ The body contours follow a '54 'deep' pattern on the back and a slightly shallower pattern at the front, preserving some body mass.

■ The body with the trem and other associated metalwork comes in at a spine-sapping 9lb 3oz compared with a typical 8lb for a '54. The body is the classic 1.75in and made of alder.

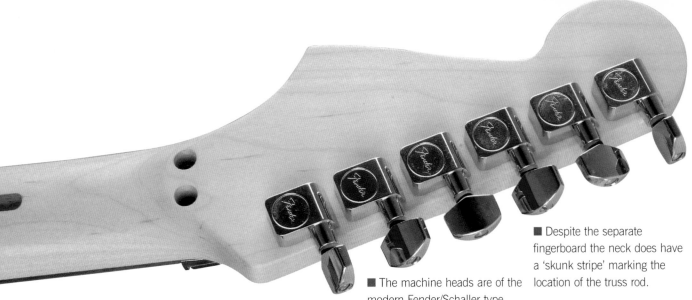

■ The neck profile follows a comfortable late '50s 'C' pattern, with a little more wood left in place near the headstock to accommodate the two bolts for the locking nut – these require a 2.5mm Allen/hex. The headstock itself has a late '50s vibe but with a recessed truss rod access.

■ The machine heads are of the modern Fender/Schaller type.

■ The fingerboard is a slab of light hardwood with a rosewood-like grain and has plastic dot markers.

■ Despite the separate fingerboard the neck does have a 'skunk stripe' marking the location of the truss rod.

■ The fingerboard and bridge set-up has a modern, flatter 9.5in radius to better facilitate string bending and a low action without excessive chocking.

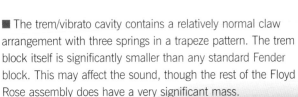

■ The trem/vibrato cavity contains a relatively normal claw arrangement with three springs in a trapeze pattern. The trem block itself is significantly smaller than any standard Fender block. This may affect the sound, though the rest of the Floyd Rose assembly does have a very significant mass.

■ There is a one-bar type string tree, which accommodates all the strings located just behind the locking nut.

■ The nut is the patented Floyd Rose locking nut, requiring two bolts directly through the guitar neck.

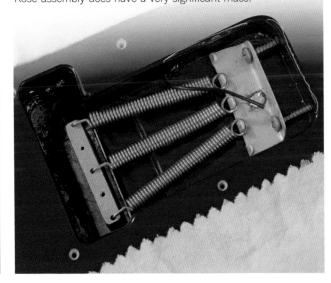

Condition on arrival

This 'new' instrument, probably made in 2005, arrived in factory mint condition except for the Floyd Rose accessories, which exhibit signs of corrosion. The chrome is flaking from the bridge saddles and bubbling at the locking nut. The set-up is generally very crude, with a distinct concave bow to the neck. Also the strap buttons are very loose. These are all correctable faults but sad to see in a Fender instrument. Leo would have been disappointed.

Specific Floyd Rose set-up – changing strings

BEWARE Do not try this on a dark stage! If you're committed to gigging with a Floyd Rose, carry a spare guitar and preferably a guitar tech. It's easy to lose some of the smaller parts of the Floyd Rose saddle clamps during a string change.

Specific routine maintenance

When you're next changing strings it's worth checking the machine-head locking nuts, which tend to work loose. On this Mexican-assembled guitar this requires a 10mm socket spanner. Do not over-tighten them – just enough to stop the machine head moving in normal use.

At the same time check the string tree – the '1' point Phillips screws also tend to work loose. This can affect tuning stability, especially when using the Floyd Rose. The all-embracing tree has a constantly variable height and should be touching the strings just enough for a downward pull on the nut but no more. Lubricating the tree underside with a little ChapStick will prevent any sticking.

The rosewood-type fingerboard tends to dry out and will benefit from a little lemon oil applied with a soft cloth – see *Contacts* in the appendix.

Whilst you have the tools out it's worth tightening the output jack retainer. This tends to work loose, causing crackles and intermittent output. Tightening sometimes entails removing the recessed jack socket using a '1' point Phillips and getting a grip on the jack retainer itself as you tighten the bolt with a 0.5in socket spanner.

If loose, the volume and tone pots also require a 0.5in socket spanner (wrench) for removal or adjustment.

1 The Fender recommendation is to use DynaMaxx FR-End strings, which have no ball ends. However, if you prefer your own brand you need to start by cutting off the ball ends with a pair of substantial wire cutters – I favour the Draper expert long-handled type as they take a lot of wear and have plenty of torque, but cheaper, smaller ones will do the job for a short while. Make a careful note of the ball end colour code for the string gauges if this information is given on the packet

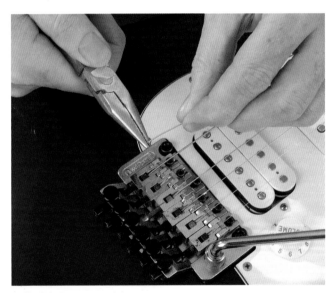

■ Before cutting any wound string always make a 90° bend in the windings to avoid any unwinding.

2 Set the fine tuners to their central position to give plenty of scope for later adjustment.

3 The old strings are removed by first de-tensioning the locking nut fasteners with a 3mm hex/Allen key. Then de-tension the strings via the machine heads as normal – Floyd Rose recommend replacing one string at a time to avoid unbalancing the trem. This is good practice on any guitar.

4 De-tension the individual hex/Allen fastener at the saddle end. I recommend a long shank 3mm key for this, as it usually requires a lot of torque. Also the long shank just clears the body, avoiding any paintwork damage – though you should take the usual precaution of positioning a rag or duster behind the saddles.

Remove the old string and de-thread it from the locking nut. The bare end of the new string can then be positioned in the block and the Allen key clamp re-tensioned. Do not over-tension, as this may damage the thread.

5 Thread the new string through the loosened locking nut and affix as normal to the machine head. Repeat for all six strings, working in from the sixth and first strings, thus maintaining an even tension on the neck. Always put a string on under tension.

6 Tune the guitar to pitch and thoroughly stretch the strings.

7 When the guitar has settled re-tension the locking nut with a 3mm hex/Allen key.

8 Recheck the tuning, this time using the fine tuners.

'Under the hood'

Removing the 11 pickguard screws using a '1' point Phillips screwdriver reveals a large 'swimming pool' rout suitable for containing any pickup arrangement up to three humbuckers.

This also reveals the countersinking of the Floyd Rose assembly bringing the bridge down to a suitable height for a conventional Strat neck/body height.

■ The tone pots are the 250K type common on single coil Strats, and these and the five-way selector have a minimal screening foil attached to the pickguard rear. The usual capacitor sits across the two tone controls.

■ The five-pole switch is of a fairly robust PCB type.

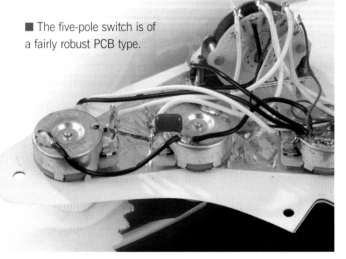

Setting the string heights

The Deluxe has a Floyd Rose bridge arrangement, which means setting the string height is a 'two point' arrangement for the whole guitar. However, the Floyd Rose is designed to offer a perfect 9.5 radius match to the neck so this should not be a problem. The overall height is adjusted via a 3mm hex/Allen key in the two pivot bolts.

The intonation adjustment for each string requires a 2.5mm Allen/hex wrench, and the saddles slide back and forth on pressing down on the tremolo arm. To correct the intonation proceed as per the Vintage Strat.

If the bridge is set very low and the action is still too high then the neck may require a little 'back angle'. The guitar features a Micro-Tilt neck, which requires a ⅛in hex wrench. This replaces the time-honoured neck shims in these modern Fenders.

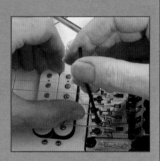

■ The pickups are two hot wound single coils and a Fender-branded humbucker. The pickup height adjustment requires a '1' point Phillips screwdriver for the single coils and a '0' point for the humbucker.

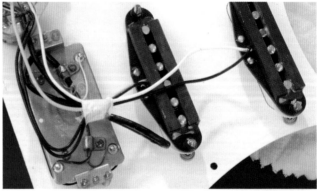

■ The rear humbucker coil offers custom setting of the individual string poles. This requires a 4mm straight blade screwdriver.

122

To adjust the neck tilt

1 Slacken the strings and loosen the two neck screws on both sides of the adjustment access hole on the neckplate by four full turns.

2 Tighten the hex/Allen key adjustment screw beneath the rear neck plate with a ⅛in wrench. A quarter-turn will raise the effective string action by approximately ½₂in.

3 Retighten the neck bolts and retune the instrument. Experiment until you achieve the desired relationship between neck tilt, saddle height, and action. See the set up notes for the Vintage Strat on page 32 and page 101 for more on this.

Signed off

The Mex was quite difficult to set up. The truss rod, which requires a ⅛in hex/Allen, would not budge at first. However, loosening the hex nuts which secure the locking nut in position seemed to release some tension in the neck and the rod turned enough to secure a fairly flat relief. The loose strap pegs were easily solved with a matchstick splinter used as a rawlplug.

Overall the guitar does what you might expect. I admit it brought out the Liverpool hooligan in me and wound up to 12 (two more!). With a little overdrive and delay I was waking up warlocks for miles. The Floyd Rose does what it says on the tin, and the wildest divebombs returned to pitch.

Indonesian-made 'Standard' Squier

A Squier Standard Series Stratocaster made in Indonesia in 2005. An unusual take on the Squier brand with several distinguishing features.

Serial No.
IC 030111753.

General description

Superficially this Strat bears a passing resemblance to a rare Vintage Stratocaster. However, a closer look reveals the body profile as ever so slightly different from the classic Strat. The pickguard is thicker than usual single-ply black plastic, with 11 larger than usual Phillips '2' slot-size screws and a bevelled edge. The one-piece black tremolo arm has an unusually large 1mm thread on a 6mm shank.

■ The body contours are of the generous Vintage 'deep' type. The body is, however, significantly lighter, with the overall guitar weight at 7.5lb compared with a typical 8.25lb for a Vintage Reissue and 8lb for an American Series. The body is the classic 1.75in (not slimmed down as with the Chinese Squier). It is probably made of Agathis wood, though the heavy coat of polyurethane makes this impossible to determine.

■ The machine heads are of the modern bolt-on Gotoh type, and distinctively black. They have adjustable resistance using a '1' point Phillips screwdriver. It's advisable to release this resistance when installing new strings.

■ The neck profile is a nice 'C' with a little more wood at the 1st position than a '57. The matching painted headstock has a late '60s/early '70s vibe – large and with a recessed truss rod access.

■ Like the American Series the fingerboard is a slab of dark hardwood with a rosewood-like grain and has 'mother of plastic' dot markers.

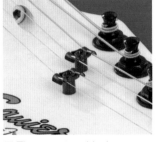

■ There are two black string trees for the first to fourth strings, of the seagull-wing type.

■ The nut is also 'mother of plastic' and measures 1.58in.

■ There is a 'skunk stripe' despite the truss rod probably being inserted before the fingerboard. The fingerboard has a modern 9.5in radius and the now standard 22 frets. The fret width is 2.4mm.

■ The body routing is more extensive and deeper than a Vintage Reissue, significantly more wood having been removed. Also the trem block has substantially less mass – it is thinner and is made from a light alloy. The block is a different shape from the Chinese Squier but with approximately the same overall mass.

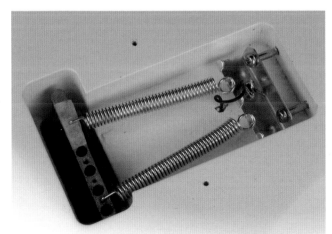

■ The trem/vibrato is viewed by removing the black rear trem cover with a Phillips '2' point screwdriver – this is of the modern 'two pivot' type, and has only two, slightly larger than usual springs.

Condition on arrival

This unusual Squier has a colour-matched headstock which in a Vintage guitar would be a very collectable feature. It also has an eye-catching black theme to its peripherals, a black one-piece trem and pickguard with matching machine heads, jack socket, trem cover, and strap buttons.

The guitar set-up was initially poor, with a very high action and slightly concave neck. Also, somewhere between here and Indonesia the strings had become very rusty.

Specific routine maintenance

When you're next changing strings it's worth checking the machine-head locking nuts, which tend to work loose. On the Indonesian Squier this requires a 10mm socket spanner. Do not over-tighten them – just enough to stop the machine head moving in normal use.

At the same time check the string trees – these are larger than usual and require a '1' point Phillips screwdriver. Loose machines will affect tuning stability, especially when using the trem/vibrato. Lubricating the tree grooves with a little Lipsalve or ChapStick prevents any sticking.

The rosewood-type fingerboard tends to dry out and will benefit from a little lemon oil – see *Contacts* in the appendix.

Whilst you have the tools out it's worth tightening the output jack retainer. This tends to work loose, causing crackles and intermittent output. Tightening sometimes entails removing the recessed jack socket using a '2' point Phillips and getting a grip on the jack retainer itself while tightening the bolt with an 11mm socket spanner.

Setting the string heights

This Standard Squier has a Vintage-type bridge arrangement but with black cast saddles as opposed to the classic pressed steel.

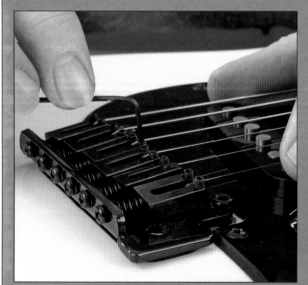

The Allen key adjustment requires a 1.54mm key. Otherwise follow the instructions for Vintage Strat action setting.

'Under the hood'

Removing the pickguard using an unusual size '2' point Phillips screwdriver reveals a large cavity able to accommodate two humbuckers and a single coil though not a 'swimming pool' arrangement. As much wood as possible has been left in situ.

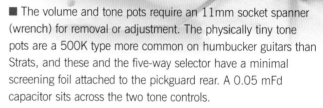

■ The volume and tone pots require an 11mm socket spanner (wrench) for removal or adjustment. The physically tiny tone pots are a 500K type more common on humbucker guitars than Strats, and these and the five-way selector have a minimal screening foil attached to the pickguard rear. A 0.05 mFd capacitor sits across the two tone controls.

■ The five-pole switch is of a PCB type common on budget guitars. This would not be ideal for extensive professional use, but is adequate in a student guitar.

■ The pickups are conventionally wound single coils with a separate pole piece (unlike the Chinese Affinity). The sound is very good. There is no mistaking the familiar Strat snap and the output is –18dB, which is what you would expect. (See the Appendix for comparative output tables.)

Signed off

The Standard Squier responded well to a minimum of attention. The truss rod needed a half-turn with a 4mm Allen/hex key, which resulted in a flattish neck with the recommended relief. The saddles were originally set too high with a random radius. This responded to the set-up as per the Vintage Strat except, of course, that the radius is 9.5in for this guitar.

The trem needed balancing but again responded easily to a typical Vintage set-up (*see page 39*).

Overall the guitar feels reasonably good. However, despite a set-up the tremolo/vibrato seems unresponsive and 'dull' – possibly due to the much lower mass in the trem block. But with a new set of strings the guitar will play well. Again this is remarkable for a budget instrument and a great testament to Leo Fender's original workmanlike plan.

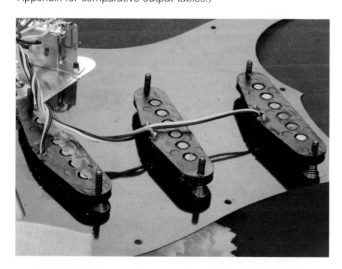

Custom Shop Eric Clapton

Made in the Fender Custom Shop, Corona, USA, on 20 January 2004. Vintage looks and hi-tech electronics combine to make an unusual Strat fit for 'Riding with the King'.

Serial No. CN 95909.

General description

Eric's Custom Shop guitar is interesting. In many ways it's a tribute to the famous original 'Blackie' that Eric used as his main guitar for many years. This was a composite guitar or 'bitsa', made from bits of several guitars. These Eric had bought second-hand in the Sho-Bud showroom in Nashville in 1970. In some ways the guitar resembles a late '50s/early '60s classic Vintage Stratocaster with a maple neck, Vintage bridge and saddles, trem in place, Kluson-type tuners, etc.

However, for his Signature guitar Eric has asked for a few changes to give him a very versatile and very modern instrument.

■ Like a '50s Strat, the pickguard is single-ply plastic with eight Phillips '1' slot-size screws. The tremolo arm takes a Vintage-type thread of 10-32 UNF on a ³⁄₁₆in shank.

■ The body contours are also of the generous Vintage 'deep' type, though more '54 than '57.

However

■ The overall guitar weight is about 8lb compared with a typical 8.25lb for a Vintage Reissue. The body is the classic 1.75in deep and is made of alder.

■ The neck profile follows Eric's favourite soft 'V', and has a satin finish to a wonderful piece of maple. The neck has a modern recessed truss rod accessed at the headstock.

■ The neck is dated 'Jan 13 2004' and pencilled 'Germany Show', which possibly refers to the Frankfurt Music Fair. The neck is a beautiful snug fit and requires no shims. The neck is fitted as always with four 1.75in woodscrews with a 1.75 thread. The guitar has no modern Micro-Tilt facility.

Condition on arrival

This new Custom Shop guitar arrived set up 'just as Eric likes them' – according to his guitar tech Lee Dickson. This means the tremolo/vibrato arrived 'blocked off', with a substantial wooden wedge behind the trem block, a screwed-down bridge plate, and five springs! However, a trem arm is supplied with the guitar should you want to put things back to normal. The inclusion of apparently redundant parts acknowledges the significant contribution of the trem block and springs to the classic Strat sound, even when the trem itself is blocked.

■ There is a 'skunk stripe', as the truss rod has been inserted from behind the fingerboard. The fingerboard has a radius of 9.5in which is mirrored beautifully at the bridge.

■ The nut looks like bone like but could be Cyclovac.

■ The fingerboard has 22 frets with the normal modern 'lip' at the neck heel and black dot markers.

■ The machine heads are of the Vintage Kluson/Fender type with the time-honoured split barrel.

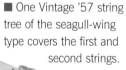

■ One Vintage '57 string tree of the seagull-wing type covers the first and second strings.

■ The trem/vibrato is of the Vintage type and has five springs. The body routing is a tad more extensive than a Vintage Reissue, a little more wood having necessarily been removed to accommodate the PP3 battery in the enlarged trem cavity. The trem block has plenty of mass, being the classic solid Vintage type found in '54s and '57s.

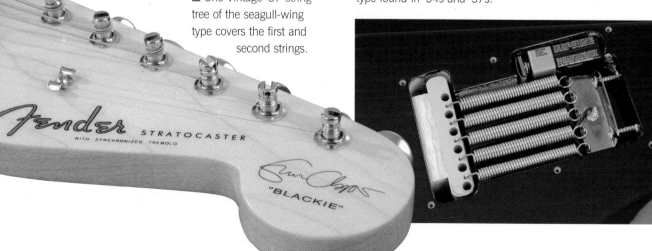

Setting the string heights

First check the neck relief with your feeler gauges. The neck should be fairly flat – perhaps .015 relief at the 7th fret (see below for more on this). If the neck does need adjustment the Clapton requires a ⅛in Allen/hex.

The Clapton has a Vintage-type bridge arrangement, with classic pressed steel saddles requiring a .050 Allen/hex for height adjustment. Otherwise follow the instructions for the Vintage Strat, similarly intonation, which requires a Phillips '1' point screwdriver.

Specific routine maintenance

The guitar is supplied with D'Addario .009/.011/.017/.026/.036/.046 strings. When you're next changing the strings, it's worth checking the Kluson screws, which tend to work loose. On the Clapton this requires a Phillips '0' point screwdriver. Do not over-tighten them – just enough to stop the machine head moving in normal use.

At the same time check the string tree – the '0' point Phillips screws also tend to work loose. This can affect tuning stability, especially when using the trem/vibrato. Lubricating the tree grooves with a little Lipsalve or ChapStick prevents sticking.

Whilst you have the tools out it's worth tightening the output jack retainer. This tends to work loose, causing crackles and intermittent output. Tightening sometimes entails removing the recessed jack socket using a '1' point Phillips and getting a grip on the jack retainer itself as you tighten the bolt with a 0.5in socket spanner.

If loose, the volume and tone pots require a 0.5in socket spanner (wrench) for removal or adjustment.

130

'Under the hood'

Removing the single-ply pickguard using a '1' point Phillips screwdriver reveals a fascinating array of quite unique electronics. The most obviously unusual feature is the 3in x 2in cut-out for the onboard preamp. This is contained on a busy little PCB with enough electronics to make a small amplifier – which is in fact what it is.

■ The usual modern five-way switch connects three slim 0.75in deep Vintage Noiseless pickups with stacked humbucking coils. The output from these is modified by an unusual set of pots. The volume pot is a 50k, then the middle tone control is in fact a dual concentric 250K and 1Meg coupled with a .022uF capacitor and 82K resistor. The second tone control is the MDX mid-boost 250K taper.

■ The pickup cavity itself is branded 'CLAPTON' and 'G' (perhaps for the Custom Shop craftsman).

The active electronics

The most startling thing about this guitar is the volume, a full 13dB louder than our reference '54. This is due, of course, to the combination of humbucking pickups and onboard pre amp.

The TBX control is a sophisticated device more at home in the studio than on stage. TBX stands for 'treble bass expander', and the control offers a normal resistive/capacitance tone control from 1–5 (centre detent at 5). Beyond 5 the control actively boosts the highs and mids.

The Clapton MDX controls also offer boost – a whopping 25dB of middle, making his favoured 'woman tone' available here on a Strat rather than a Les Paul.

I particularly like the way all this hi tech is made invisible on a guitar with an outwardly Vintage vibe.

Signed off

As supplied the Clapton needed no attention at all. Eric likes them as they come from the Custom Shop. So if this one has retained that set-up then the first string is set at a comfortable .010in at the first string and .016in at the sixth (17th fret), with .013 first string and .016 sixth string at the first fret. The consequent neck relief is approximately .015 at the 7th fret whilst fretted at the 17th.

Overall the guitar sounds very good acoustically. Like all good electric instruments it also plays like a guitar before any electricity or electronics are involved.

USA-made '74 Vintage Reissue

Serial No. V00938

Made in 2005, this guitar represents a typical example of the current Fender reissues of their CBS era Stratocasters. It has been built to closely resemble a guitar produced in the 1970s, minus, however, any of the defects often rightly or wrongly attributed to that period of Fender history.

General description
This may look like any other Stratocaster, but a closer look reveals some attention to authentic '70s detail.

■ The five-way switch knob is an alternative offered with this model, though the three-way switch would have still been standard at this time.

■ The pickup covers are sharp at the edges, following the pattern adopted in 1955–6.

■ The pickguard is triple-ply white plastic with 11 Phillips '1' slot-size screws. The tremolo arm has a 10-32 UNF thread on a ³⁄₁₆in shank and has the moderate angle adopted in the late '50s.

■ The bridge has six pressed steel saddles with the 'Fender' stamp. The saddles require the expected .050 Allen for height adjustment. The string length adjustment requires the usual Vintage '1' point Phillips head.

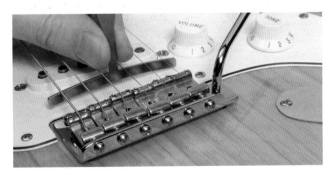

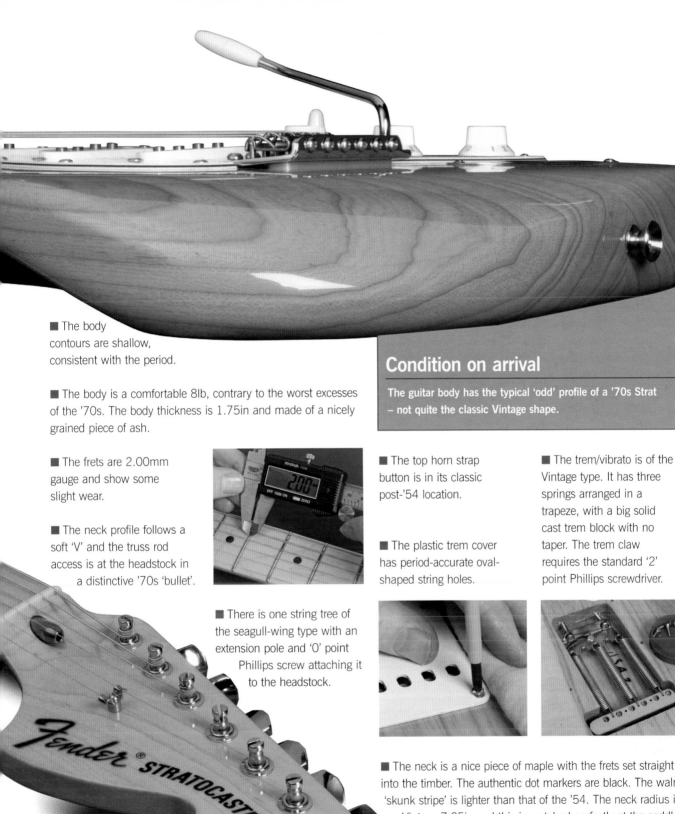

■ The body contours are shallow, consistent with the period.

■ The body is a comfortable 8lb, contrary to the worst excesses of the '70s. The body thickness is 1.75in and made of a nicely grained piece of ash.

■ The frets are 2.00mm gauge and show some slight wear.

■ The neck profile follows a soft 'V' and the truss rod access is at the headstock in a distinctive '70s 'bullet'.

■ There is one string tree of the seagull-wing type with an extension pole and '0' point Phillips screw attaching it to the headstock.

■ The nut is a well-cut piece of bone-like plastic, probably Cyclovac.

Condition on arrival

The guitar body has the typical 'odd' profile of a '70s Strat – not quite the classic Vintage shape.

■ The top horn strap button is in its classic post-'54 location.

■ The plastic trem cover has period-accurate oval-shaped string holes.

■ The trem/vibrato is of the Vintage type. It has three springs arranged in a trapeze, with a big solid cast trem block with no taper. The trem claw requires the standard '2' point Phillips screwdriver.

■ The neck is a nice piece of maple with the frets set straight into the timber. The authentic dot markers are black. The walnut 'skunk stripe' is lighter than that of the '54. The neck radius is a Vintage 7.25in and this is matched perfectly at the saddles except for the low E, which is set slightly higher.

■ The machine heads are the ageing Fender/Kluson type made by Schaller, but so far no gear teeth are missing and they work just fine. The real '70s machines, I'm reliably informed, had a nasty habit of falling apart.

Specific routine maintenance

First check the neck relief with your feeler gauges. The neck should be fairly flat – perhaps .015 relief at the 7th fret. If the neck relief does need adjustment the '74 requires a ⅛in Allen. For more on neck relief and truss rod adjustment follow the Vintage Strat set up guide similarly for any saddle adjustment and intonation adjustments see page 32-37.

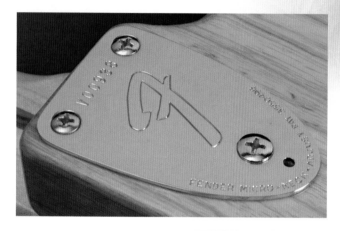

When changing strings, which are .010s on this guitar, it's worth checking the machine-head fixing screws, which tend to work loose. On the '74 this requires a '1' point Phillips. Do not over-tighten them – just enough to stop the machine head moving in normal use.

The '70s saw the introduction of the Micro-Tilt neck adjustment on a three-bolt neck. This requires a ³⁄₃₂in Allen. See page 101 for more on Micro-Tilt adjustment.

At the same time check the string tree – the '0' point Phillips screw also tends to vibrate loose. This can affect tuning stability, especially when using the trem/vibrato. Lubricating the underneath of the seagull with a little Vaseline or ChapStick will prevent any sticking.

Whilst you have the tools out it's worth tightening the output jack retainer. This tends to work loose, causing crackles and intermittent output. Tightening sometimes entails removing the recessed jack socket using a '1' point Phillips and getting a grip on the jack retainer itself as you tighten the bolt with a 0.5in socket spanner.

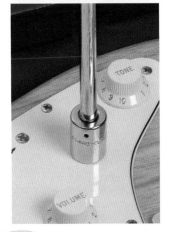

'Under the hood'

Removing the pickguard using the usual '1' point Phillips screwdriver reveals a beautifully clean rout. The minimum of wood has been removed, returning to the original Fender concept of 'a railway sleeper with strings'. Remember the 'other' use for the Fender 'ashtray' as a screw retainer.

■ The heavily wound pickups in their '71 cases have rubber washers instead of the later springs for fixing their height from the fingerboard.

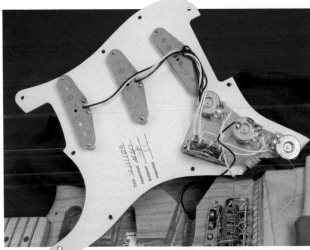

■ If loose, the volume and tone pots require a 0.5in socket spanner (wrench) for removal or adjustment.

■ The wiring is impeccable, with three classic 250K pots and a '70s-type 0.05mF capacitor routed via a three-way switch. All the wire seems to be a wax-coated cloth.

■ The only electrical screening is a thick metal plate confined to the area above the potentiometers.

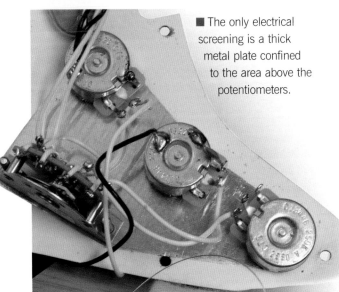

Signed off

I was pleasantly surprised by this guitar. Though it initially awakened all my prejudices against this period of manufacture it actually turned out to be a fine playing instrument. The natural finished ash looks great. Fender are working hard to set the record straight.

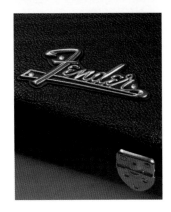

Japanese-made 50th Anniversary

A good example of the excellent guitars produced by Fender Japan. Aside from the rosewood fingerboard and the humbucker body rout this stands up very well next to the Corona made '57 re-issue.

Serial No. V 009320.

General description

For the 50th anniversary Fender Japan chose to celebrate a high point in Stratocaster history – the pre-1960 and pre-CBS rosewood fingerboard custom colour guitar. The first black Strat had in fact appeared in 1955, but this replica has a 'slab' fingerboard with a flat rear profile, so its role model perhaps dated to 1959, the first official year for rosewood-fingerboard Strats.

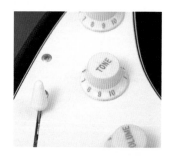

■ The aged pickguard is triple ply plastic with 11 Phillips '1' point screws, while the tremolo arm takes a vintage-type thread of 10-32 UNF on a ³⁄₁₆in shank. However, the tremolo arm is currently missing in action.

■ The body contours are generally of the Vintage 'deep' type. However, they're slightly eccentric – very in keeping with the late '50s, when hand-sanding produced varied results depending on who was doing it at the time. The rear contour is more generous at the neck end than on my '57 and the front contour less so.

■ The guitar is heavy, with the overall weight at about 9lb compared with a typical 8.25lb for a Vintage reissue. The body depth is the classic 1.75in. It's possibly made of alder, though the heavy coat of black polyurethane makes this impossible to determine.

■ The neck profile follows a comfortable 'U' pattern – chunkier, however, than that found on the American-made '57 reissue. The headstock has a late '50s/early '60s vibe.

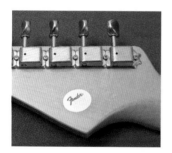 

■ The machine heads are of the classic Kluson type.

■ The Fender decal has the 'Spaghetti' logo and 'with synchronised tremolo', but no patent number – a style followed up to 1960.

■ The one string tree is of the Vintage seagull-wing type.

■ The fingerboard is a slab of dark hardwood with a rosewood-like grain and 'mother of plastic' dot markers. This feature places the replica firmly in the late 1959/early 1960 era. The nut is also aged plastic.

Condition on arrival

'Fender Japan' was established in 1982 to deal head-on with competition from the Far East. Given their impeccable standards of manufacture, Japanese Fenders were very soon as good and often better than their American originals. Indeed, for a short time following the management buyout of 1985 only Japanese Fenders were available, Fender having lost their own factory site during the repurchase!

Our case study guitar is part of a batch issued to celebrate Fender's 50th anniversary in 1996. The neck date confirms this, and finding it also reveals an unusual shim in the base of the neck socket.

This guitar pre-empts the later 'closet classics' with its artificially aged plastic parts, these having a perhaps slightly overdone greenish-brown tinge meant to evoke a finish reminiscent of too many gigs in smoky bars in downtown Osaka. Other than that the condition is 'as new'. Ironically, with real wear and tear some of the fake patina is rubbing off, and the tone knobs are 'ageing' white!

The saddles are presently a little low, causing slight string choking on the first and second strings.

Outwardly this is a nice guitar with a good late '50s vibe.

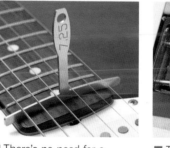 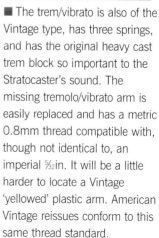

■ There's no need for a 'skunk stripe' as the truss rod has been inserted before the fingerboard. The fingerboard has a vintage radius of 7.25in.

■ The trem/vibrato is also of the Vintage type, has three springs, and has the original heavy cast trem block so important to the Stratocaster's sound. The missing tremolo/vibrato arm is easily replaced and has a metric 0.8mm thread compatible with, though not identical to, an imperial 5⁄32in. It will be a little harder to locate a Vintage 'yellowed' plastic arm. American Vintage reissues conform to this same thread standard.

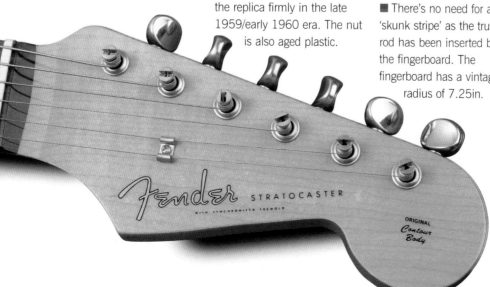

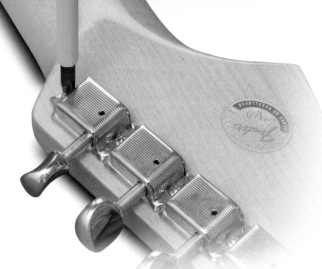

Specific routine maintenance

When you're next changing strings it's worth checking the machine head screws, which tend to work loose. On the Japanese Strat this requires a '1' point Phillips screwdriver. Do not over-tighten them – just enough to stop the machine head moving in normal use.

At the same time check the string tree. The '0' point Phillips screw also tends to work loose, and this can affect tuning stability, especially when using the trem/vibrato.

Setting the string heights

The Japanese Strat has a Vintage-type bridge arrangement with the classic pressed steel saddles. The Allen key string height adjustment requires a 1.54mm key. Otherwise follow the text for 'Bridge adjustment, Part 1: Setting the string heights' (see page 32).

Lubricating the tree grooves with a little petroleum lip ointment such as ChapStick or Lipsalve also prevents string-sticking.

The rosewood-type fingerboard tends to dry out and will benefit from the application of a little lemon oil on a clean lint-free cloth. (See *Contacts* in the Appendix.)

Whilst you have the tools out it's worth tightening the output jack retainer. This tends to work loose, causing crackles and intermittent output. Tightening sometimes entails removing the recessed jack socket using a '1' point Phillips and getting a grip on the jack retainer itself while tightening the bolt with an 11mm socket spanner.

'Under the hood'

Removing the pickguard using a '1' point Phillips screwdriver reveals a modern versatile cavity able to accommodate two humbuckers, in the neck and bridge positions. This rather dispels any Vintage illusions. The humbucker slots have been further part-excavated to reduce the body weight.

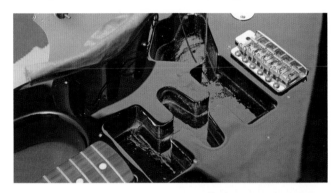

■ The five-pole switch is of the square PCB type common on budget guitars. This would not be ideal for extensive professional use, but is adequate.

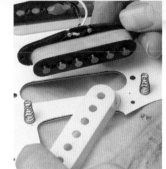

■ The pickups are regular Strat-type single coils but quite heavily wound.

■ There's also a strange anomaly in the neck cut-out consisting of two half-round cuts. These don't seem to cause any specific problem and may simply be another attempt to reduce the body weight.

■ The tone pots are a physically tiny 250K type, and these and the five-way selector have a minimal screening foil attached to the pickguard rear. A 0.1mFd capacitor sits across the two tone controls. The wiring is modern PVC, spoiling the Vintage effect but probably perfectly effective.

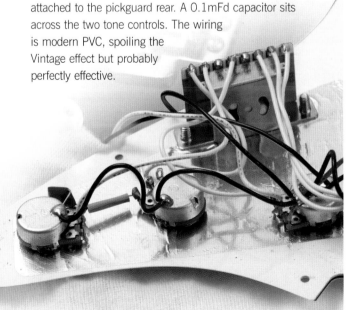

Signed off

The Japanese Strat responded well to a minimum of attention. The saddles were originally set too low with a random radius. This responded to a set-up using the 7.25in radius gauge.

The tremolo/vibrato needed balancing but again responded easily to a typical Vintage set-up. The nut, which was a little sticky, resulted in some pinging when tuning, but this was easily cured with a little graphite in the slots. If a pencil doesn't do it then a little fine graphite lock lubricant bound with Vaseline will.

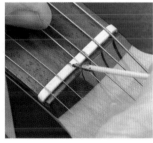

The intonation was slightly off but responded easily to a Vintage set-up, as described in 'Bridge adjustment, Part 2: Setting the working string length' (see page 35).

The saddles on the first and second strings were prone to a mechanical rattle but a little Loctite on the grub screw threads tightened these. This glue will never actually stick steel to steel in this situation but the residue provides enough resistance to stop the rattle.

Overall the guitar feels good and makes a fairly convincing N.O.S. as long as you don't look too close. I should think the 50th anniversary guitars will eventually become collectors' items.

Fender American Series 2005

The Fender guitar in its current specification.
A design classic slightly updated to cope with
the rigours of 21st Century stage conditions.

Serial No. Z4032031.

General description

This American-made Strat has in many ways returned to
Leo's original concept and has a close similarity to the classic
'improved' Stratocaster of the early '60s. To the casual viewer
there is little significant visual difference. The fingerboard is,
triple-ply plastic with eleven Phillips '1' size screws
rather than eight. See the appendix for
precise screw sizes.

■ The body contours are in some ways deeper than our 1954
example, but the top contour cuts into the centre of the body
less, thus preserving more actual body mass.

This contouring stems from Leo's original consultations with
Bill Carson and other early Fender players, who often
complained that the Telecaster's slab body could dig into your
ribs. The new design takes this further on the important back
edge. However, the front 'elbow' contour is slightly less
pronounced, again preserving some body mass.

■ The overall guitar weight comes in at about 8lb compared with a typical 8.25lb for a Vintage Reissue. A little weight is lost in the pickup routing, which can accommodate single coil or parallel coil humbuckers. The body thickness is the classic 1.75in and is made of alder, though this guitar is also offered in the original ash as a custom order.

■ There is one 'easy glide' string tree for the first and second strings.

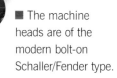

■ The neck profile follows a comfortable early '60s type 'C' profile. The headstock has a late '50s vibe but with a recessed truss rod access.

■ The nut is bone, or a very good imitation, probably Cyclovac. The modern nut and neck are slightly wider than the 'vintage' width – as shown.

■ The machine heads are of the modern bolt-on Schaller/Fender type.

■ The fingerboard is a slab of dark rosewood with white clay-type dot markers.

■ There is no need for a 'skunk stripe', as the truss rod has been inserted before the fingerboard. The fingerboard has a larger 9.5in radius to facilitate string bending without choking.

■ Access to the trem/vibrato is via a new triple-ply access cover with a large single cavity string port. The trem is of the 'improved' type, and has three black metal springs arranged in a parallel array rather than the fan arrangement found in many vintage guitars. The trem 'block' itself is thinner and more sophisticated in its casting.

Tech Tip

Sometimes you get trouble with the factory-fitted Fender 'Bullet' strings jamming in the trem block. These can be released by gently tapping on a small Allen key inserted from the top of the guitar through the saddle.

Andy Gibson – Guitar Tech

Specific routine maintenance

When you're next changing strings it's worth checking the machine head locking nuts. On the American Series this requires a 10mm socket spanner. Do not over-tighten them – just enough to stop the machine head moving in normal use.

The machine heads themselves have a tension adjustment requiring a 4mm flathead screwdriver. One of these particular Schallers had worked loose and had a little play in it.

The rosewood-type fingerboard tends to dry out and will benefit from a little lemon oil applied with a soft cloth. (See *Contacts* in appendix.)

It's worth taking the opportunity to remove the debris that tends to accumulate around the frets. This black 'gunk' is largely a mixture of sweat and dead skin and should come away easily with the help of a softwood cocktail stick as a gentle persuader.

Whilst you have the tools out it's also worth tightening the output jack retainer. This tends to work loose, causing crackles and intermittent output.

At the same time check the string tree. The '0' point Phillips screw tends to work loose and this can affect tuning stability, especially when using the trem/vibrato.

Lubricating the tree grooves with a little petroleum lip ointment such as ChapStick or Lipsalve also prevents string-sticking and aids stable tuning.

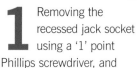

■ If the socket is very loose tightening sometimes entails:

1 Removing the recessed jack socket using a '1' point Phillips screwdriver, and

2 Getting a grip on the jack retainer itself as you tighten the bolt with a 0.5in socket spanner (wrench).

Setting the string heights

The American Series has a Vintage-type bridge arrangement but with compressed stainless steel saddles as opposed to the classic pressed steel.

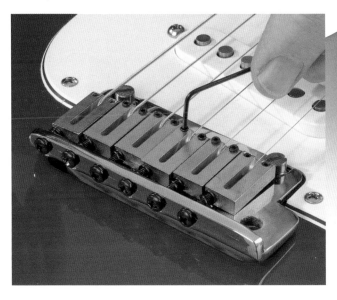

The Allen key string height adjustment requires a Vintage .050 key and the string length adjustment a Phillips '1' point screwdriver, so follow the 'step-by-step' text for Vintage Strat intonation and height adjustment.

NB: The bridge saddle radius should follow the new neck radius of 9.5in, not 7.25in. Use Stewmac radius guides (illustated).

Alternatively make a cardboard template based on the outline of your fingerboard radius to check this.

■ Shims

One refinement originally introduced on some of the three-bolt '70s Fender necks is the replacement of the rather crude neck shims with a mechanical Micro-Tilt arrangement. Both methods serve the same purpose, that of tilting the neck back slightly, thus amending the angle of the strings to the fingerboard. The telltale sign that this may be required is when the bridge saddles are set at a minimum height and the overall string action is still a little high.

■ To adjust the neck tilt

1 Slacken the strings, slowly and carefully spreading the tension loss evenly by unwinding first and sixth strings then second and fifth, etc – sudden changes in neck tension can cause problems, so don't tempt fate. For a stable guitar I recommend you never cut through all the tensioned strings with a wire cutter! Leave this to people who don't own the guitars they're restringing.

2 Using a point '2' Phillips screwdriver, loosen the two neck screws on both sides of the adjustment access hole on the neckplate by four full turns.

3 Tighten the hex/Allen key adjustment screw beneath the rear neck plate with a ⅛in wrench. A quarter-turn will raise the effective string action by approximately ¹⁄₃₂in.

4 Re-tighten the neck bolts and retune the instrument. Experiment until you achieve the desired relationship between neck tilt, saddle height, and string action.

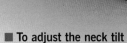

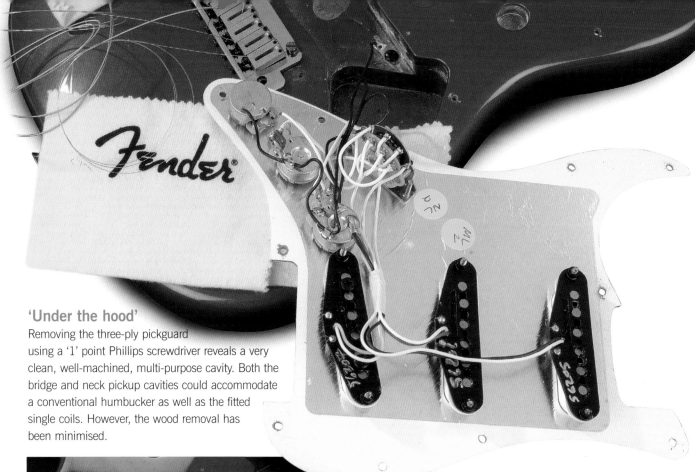

'Under the hood'

Removing the three-ply pickguard using a '1' point Phillips screwdriver reveals a very clean, well-machined, multi-purpose cavity. Both the bridge and neck pickup cavities could accommodate a conventional humbucker as well as the fitted single coils. However, the wood removal has been minimised.

■ The pickups are American Standard single coils with a custom magnet stagger designed to cope more evenly with a plain third string arrangement. The neck pickup is specified slightly hotter and the centre pickup is reverse-wired/reverse-polarity to achieve a hum-cancelling effect in the 'combined' switch positions. These pickups produce more output than the Vintage '54 Strat, thus improving the signal-to-noise ratio even in a single coil position. However, it's worth noting that this difference only amounts to 4dBA (PPM) – the smallest change the average untrained human ear can detect is approximately 3dBA, so we're not talking huge differences.

■ The wiring is very tidy and the soldering, though over-fluxed, is solid. The tone and volume pots are a 250K type. An MP .022uF capacitor sits across the two tone controls, while the bottom tone control has the 'Delta tone' facility detent. This removes the capacitor from the circuit, giving you a 'hot-wire' direct to the pickups.

■ The tone control works for both the middle and bridge pickups. This breaks the Vintage tradition of having no tone circuit on the bridge pickup, but the detent effectively restores that possibility if required. A more conventional approach applies to the neck tone control. The professional quality 'five-way pickup selector' and the general wiring benefit from an overall screening foil attached to the pickguard rear.

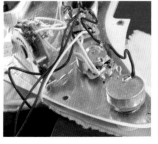

■ If loose, the volume and tone pots require a 0.5in socket spanner for removal or adjustment.

Signed off

The American responded well to a minimum of attention. The truss rod required a quarter turn, which resulted in a flattish neck with the Fender recommended relief. The saddles were set correctly with an appropriate 9.5in radius.

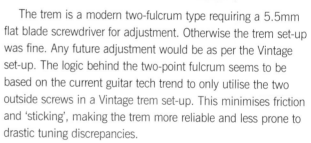

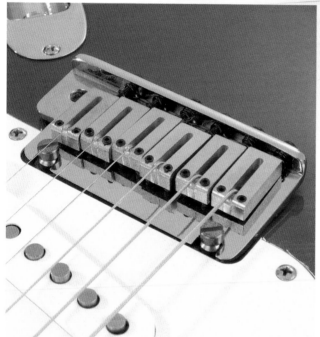

The trem is a modern two-fulcrum type requiring a 5.5mm flat blade screwdriver for adjustment. Otherwise the trem set-up was fine. Any future adjustment would be as per the Vintage set-up. The logic behind the two-point fulcrum seems to be based on the current guitar tech trend to only utilise the two outside screws in a Vintage trem set-up. This minimises friction and 'sticking', making the trem more reliable and less prone to drastic tuning discrepancies.

Overall the guitar feels terrific, very solid and well engineered. Just a little tasteful refinement of a classic design.

Chinese 'Standard' Squier

This guitar is very similar to the other Chinese 'Affinity' Squier already featured and therefore doesn't merit a full case study. However, this guitar provided our test bed for pickup, switch, and pot replacement (see appropriate chapters). It also required a certain amount of 'setting up' which proved interesting.

Serial No.
CY21216136.

General description

The features that do distinguish this guitar from the Affinity are:

- A full-depth body (1.75in).

- Full specification single coil pickups (no bar magnet).

- A different cast metal approach to the bridge saddles.

- A two-pivot 'modern' trem.

- A 22nd fret.

- Trem spring access with the plastic cover in place.

However, as new it did present some set up issues that are likely to be of interest. John Diggins took a look at the guitar after a month's use and observed:

- Some excess relief in the neck, easily solved by a truss rod adjustment.

- More seriously some rather uneven fretting – putting this right could cost as much as 50 per cent of the purchase price of the guitar, so buyers beware!

Fret correction: a professional approach

1 John sited the neck and immediately spotted the problem.

2 The 'proud' frets were isolated with a straight edge.

3 Placing the neck on his jig, John first brought the proud frets down to the correct height with a specialist diamond-coated fret stone.

4 The debris was then cleared with a soft brush.

5 A specially shaped fret stone was used to dress the profile of the lowered frets.

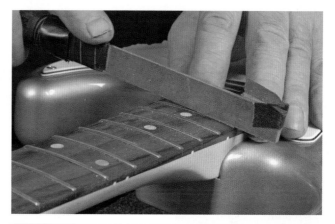

6 The dressed frets were then polished with a very fine abrasive paper.

7 John then finished the polishing using an electric buffer.

8 The opportunity was also taken to clear some debris from the fret shoulders using a wooden cocktail stick.

9 After this the rosewood fingerboard was treated to a light cleaning and 'feeding' with some high quality lemon oil.

Signed Off

The Standard Squier is now a reasonably good instrument. However, the low cost saddle materials and the lightweight trem block mean the guitar has significantly less sustain than a full-blown Strat. A good student instrument.

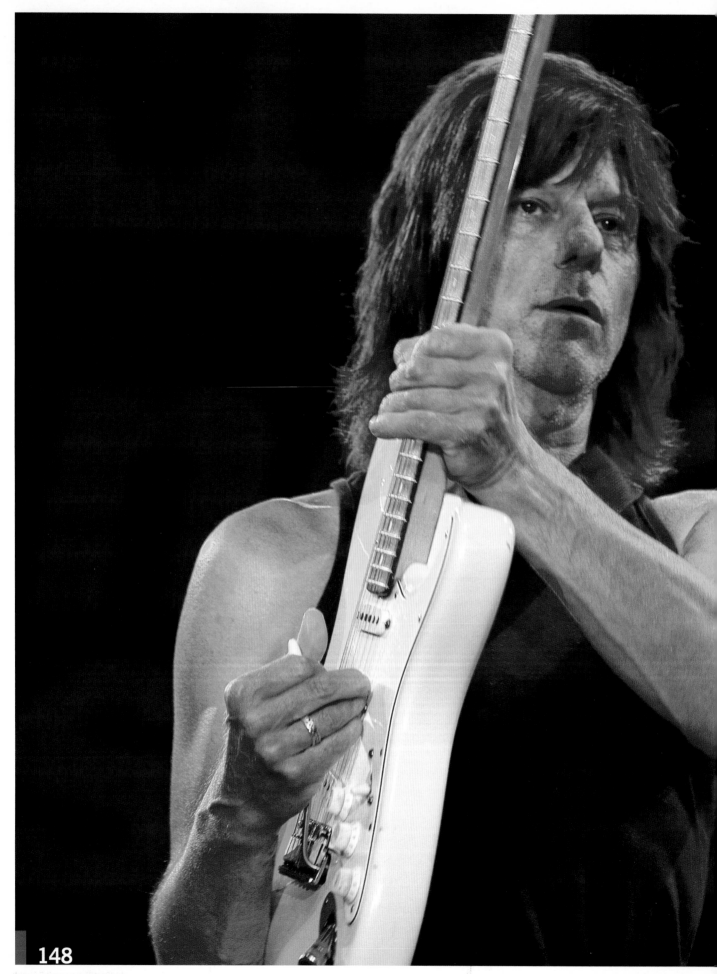

Key Strat players and their guitars

The question: Can we learn something about Strat mythology from analysing and thereby allocating a place in the equation for the scientific and measurable factors?

The Stratocaster has become one of the most potent icons of popular music history. Fifty plus years after its invention, this unique instrument still prevails over all imitators, so what makes the Strat so special? And are all Strats essentially the same, much as Leo Fender intended?

Analysing some legendary Stratocaster sounds and more importantly their players' approach to sound, can we come a little nearer to understanding the mythology that surrounds some of these instruments? What are the practical realities that make a particular instrument so inspiring for an individual musician at a specific time in their career?

We start with the inspired musician and develop from his original idea to the guitar itself. There are then as many as ten stages in the sound chain, often involving other important creative individuals such as the guitar tech, the sound engineer, and the record producer. This applies as much today to live sound as it once did to recording, as so much studio-originated sound technology has now found its way into the live amphitheatre.

LEFT Jeff Beck and his Signature Strat

RIGHT Eric Clapton's 'Blackie'.

Buddy Holly

Buddy Holly was amongst the first pop singers to realise the potential of the Strat. Leo Fender had initially designed his guitar with the needs of 'Country' and 'Western Swing' players firmly in mind.

What Buddy realised before almost anybody else was the 'style' potential of this instrument, which was outrageous for the late '50s. But Buddy also realised that this guitar was much more than a louder acoustic guitar – it had a sound character as distinct as its looks.

The guitar pictured is Buddy's last Strat, like his others a 'straight out of the box' guitar for 1958. It weighs 8lb and has a standard maple neck and all factory-standard parts.

The Holly sound is what you expect to get when you plug a standard Vintage Strat into a Fender 'tube' amp and play full first position chords all in typical Buddy Holly down strokes with a plastic or tortoiseshell plectrum.

This 'electric rhythm' sound and the guitar's outrageous shape became an important part of Buddy's whole persona. It's possible this sound even influenced the songs, which grew out of that 'attitude'. What we are left with is a heritage of perfect pop songs with 'Fender guitar' stamped on their sound world. Of course, everything he did with his Strat would have worked perfectly well on his acoustic Martin. However, when played on his Strat it had a new energy, a modernity that was shocking, vibrant, and today still encapsulates the spirit of an era.

One innovation that seems so obvious now is Buddy's use of Leo's switchable pickups for timbre contrast within a song. The best-known example is Buddy's famous pickup change for the chordal solo in the recorded version of 'Peggy Sue'. To achieve the classic change to the bridge pickup for the solo before the days of footswitch operated multi-channel amps, Buddy recruited Niki Sullivan to make the change for him. This left Buddy's right hand free and enabled him to keep his insistent rhythm driving across the change of tone colour.

'Peggy Sue' was recorded in mono straight 'as live' to analogue tape.

The Buddy Holly guitar sound we now take for granted was a novelty in 1957/8, and the fact that it now sounds so normal is a simple example of synergy and musical magic.

Eric Clapton 1

'Brownie' – a 1956 Sunburst Stratocaster serial no 12073

Perhaps most famously associated with the searing guitar riff of 'Layla', this Stratocaster could have been Buddy Holly's guitar. This reminds us how versatile Leo Fender's invention has become, and also how important a player's individual approach to technique and amplification can be to apparently transforming the Strat sound.

As a sign of the changing fortunes of the Strat, Eric bought this one from London's Sound City, 124 Charing Cross Road, in May 1967 for £150. It recently sold at Sotheby's for $497,500!

The only crucial difference between this guitar and Buddy Holly's is Eric's decision to 'lock off' the tremolo/vibrato, effectively making the guitar a 'hard tail' Strat (see *Hard Tail options* page 78). To this day he prefers the trem to be fitted to his guitars and then blocked off, rightly

believing that the trem assembly with its mass of metal and springs has a significant effect on the sound of the instrument.

Eric is a stickler for detail, insisting on the 'old-fashioned' pressed steel bridge saddles rather than the 'new improved' solid steel variety found on more recent Strats.

For amplification during the 'Layla' period Eric favoured a Fender Champ, a 6W amplifier with an 8in speaker! Eric liked the practice amp's ability to achieve classic overdrive sounds at very low volume. His 'tweed' version of the amp featured one volume control, which also functioned as an on/off switch. This was definitely Eric's minimalist period. On stage at the time he used a slightly more powerful Fender Showman.

The classic 'Layla' recording took place in 1970 at Atlantic South-Criteria Studios, Miami, Florida. The engineers were Ron Albert, Chuck Kirkpatrick, and Howie Albert, with the legendary Tom Dowd producing. It was recorded to multitrack analogue tape, a few overdubs were added, and it was then mixed down to analogue stereo.

Hank Marvin

1958 Fiesta Red Stratocaster serial no 34346

This is generally accepted as the first UK Strat. It produced the sound heard on 'Apache' and several other No 1 instrumental hits.

The story of how Hank Marvin of Cliff Richard's then backing group The Shadows came to be in possession of the only UK Fender Stratocaster in 1958 has often been told (see, for instance, *17 Watts* by Mo Foster, published by Sanctuary Press). For our purposes the important sound elements are these:

■ A top-of-the-line 'gold-plated' maple neck Fiesta Red Fender Stratocaster with heavy gauge burnished strings including a then normal wound third. (I'm sure the Fiesta Red paint makes a difference to how you play a guitar! A polite Sunburst Strat would never make such an outrageous sound!)

■ A British-made VOX AC 15 or AC 30 valve amplifier designed by Tom Jennings and Dick Denney of Jennings Musical Instruments (JMI), founded in 1958 in Dartford, Kent. Within a couple of years of VOX's initial introduction of the AC 15 Hank would ask Dick for something more powerful, resulting in the well-known AC 30. The Shadows received theirs in late '59. This was a Class 1 amplifier with huge and heavy transformers, producing a warm and powerful predominantly 'clean' guitar sound with just a touch of subtle valve distortion, compression, and very subtle 'crunch' distortion on transient peaks. This distinctive amplifier remains in production in the 21st century. The early ones were so heavy that the handles invariably broke under the strain! The valves became very hot in use and kept the van warm on the way back from cold winter gigs.

■ The AC 30 featured a quad configuration of EL84s, a larger power transformer, a heavy-duty GZ34 rectifier, and two specially toughened 12in 15W Celestion G12 speakers which became known as VOX 'Blues'.

■ A Meazzi Echomatic echo box. This valve powered tape loop recorder/player was the source of a fantastic variety of repeat 'echoes' and double tracks. This was accomplished by recording on a ¼in magnetic tape loop and immediately playing it back on several spaced playback heads.

"No one touched it for a while – they just stared, amazed"
Hank Marvin

The early Meazzi models featured five equally-spaced playback heads, and one more distantly spaced 'echo' head. The sound could be infinitely varied by mixing the outputs of the various tape heads and feeding some playback sound to the record head. The device originated in Italy, and Hank had been introduced to the Meazzi by fellow guitarist Joe Brown. Joe was apparently unimpressed by the device but Hank saw the potential for a 'slapback echo' as heard on so many American records, such as Elvis Presley's recordings at Sun featuring studio-created tape echo effects.

Hank went immediately to Jenning's Shop in London's Charing Cross Road and acquired a Meazzi, by then imported and badged as a VOX device.

For the historic 'Apache' session Hank apparently switched off the second Meazzi playback head to create the distinctive delay followed by quicker staggered repeats.

A detailed analysis of Hank's use of analogue tape and also 'drum'-type Binson delays has been carried out by programmer Charlie Hall and recreated digitally as the Alesis QuadraVerb 2/Q20 with 'Echoes From The Past'. The Alesis Q20 (which superseded the original QuadraVerb 2 and is now, unfortunately, no longer in production) could be loaded with a suite of programs from 'Echoes From The Past'. Charlie Hall's analysis and replication of vintage echoes are extremely accurate and authentic. Anyone who is interested in this particular sound should investigate an Alesis QuadraVerb 2 or Q20 with 'Echoes From The Past' programming. A Q20 is the more desirable unit, as it has a larger internal memory and is therefore capable of more accurate simulations than the earlier QuadraVerb 2. 'Echoes From The Past' have now moved to platforms such as the ZOOM RFX2200.

Another often overlooked factor is the reverb facilities at Abbey Road Studios. By 1960 Studio 2 would have had access to excellent valve-powered EMT reverb plates, as well as real tiled 'echo rooms' featuring valve mikes and amplifiers – all of this under the supervision of engineer Malcolm Addey and the most successful British producer of the time, Norrie Paramor. I myself worked with Norrie for several years and know he also favoured a 'first reflection' tape delay inserted before any reverb sends from the mixing desk.

Malcolm Addey had this to say (in November 2003's *Sound on Sound*) when commenting on an earlier session for Cliff Richard's 'Move It': 'We had an EMI RS1 mono desk with two-band, Pultec-type peaking EQ on each of its eight inputs – as opposed to the classically oriented shelving EQ that was to be found in the other studios – at 5kHz and 100Hz. There was also an echo send for all of the inputs, echo return, a peak level

ABOVE The Strat in 1958 with its original owner.
OPPOSITE The first 'British' Strat.

meter and a single main gain control. The monitor speaker, positioned to the left of the console, was a Tannoy 15-inch dual-concentric mounted inside a large bass reflex enclosure and driven by the power amp built into an EMI BTR2 mono tape machine. Running at 15ips, this served as the main recorder while another BTR2 stood by in case there was a need to do mono-to-mono overdubs.

'Meanwhile, a third machine running at 30ips took care of the delay going into the echo chamber. This was an L-shaped room located behind the north wall of the studio, with brick walls, reinforced concrete ceiling and floor, and a half-dozen glazed ceramic drainpipes that stood vertically and were positioned around the chamber to help scatter the sound. A Neumann KM53 omnidirectional mike was placed at one end of the room, while at the other end, pointing slightly upwards and towards a corner, there was a Tannoy 15-inch dual-concentric speaker driven by a Leak TL25 amp.'

Perhaps the most crucial element as ever was the unique genius of musician Hank Marvin. Hank took a tuneful riff-based melody, written and played to him on a ukulele by writer Gerry Lordan, and turned all the above elements into a classic Stratocaster hit 'Apache'.

Completists should know that Hank's Strat was perfectly complemented by Jet Harris's Fender Precision Bass and Bruce Welch's Gibson J200. Cliff Richard supplied the J200 and played the tom-tom intro!

The Beatles

Two Sonic Blue Stratocasters from 1961

(George's serial no 83840 – John's serial no unknown)

Though The Beatles visual image is closely associated with Gretsch and Rickenbacker guitars George Harrison had always admired the distinctive Fender Stratocaster sound. When Strats were rare in the UK in the early '60's, he had come tantalisingly close to acquiring one from a German source. However, he was pipped at the post by another Liverpool guitarist also working the Hamburg scene and had to make do with a Gretsch Duo Jet. This serves as a reminder of how coveted 'real' Strats were in Europe until the mid '60's especially outside of London. The lack of a Fender didn't stop George penning his Shadows influenced instrumental 'Cry for a Shadow'.

In 1965 however, George and John Lennon acquired two 'Sonic Blue' Stratocasters. The Beatles were obviously too famous to shop themselves at this point and dispatched their roadie Mal Evans to fetch a couple. Its interesting that the wealthy Beatles bought two 'second-hand' Strats. George's no. 83840 has a neck dated as 1961. Ironically by the mid sixties Strats were very unfashionable in England so new ones may have been hard to find.

The Strats were used extensively on the Beatles 'Rubber Soul' and 'Revolver' albums. The song 'Nowhere Man' features a particularly classic Strat sound, 'clean' with a bit of edge derived from a slightly overdriven valve amplifier probably a VOX AC 30 (see Hank Marvin) or possibly a Blackface Fender Showman utilising two 7025, one 2AX7 and four 6L6GC valves. According to George the solo on 'Nowhere Man' features the two Strats played in unison, the second lead guitarist being John.

This solo is a brilliant example of the synergy that occurs when Leo's genius guitar design is at the service of musical genius. I have admired this solo for years as a brilliant miniature. It is short, melodic and effective, making the most of very little. For this book I thought I should learn to play the solo in order to write in a more informed way. Confronted with the written music I couldn't believe how little substance the solo contained. However, the three simple arpeggios combined with a portamento slide, ending with an open bottom E and a high E harmonic fit the Strat like a hand-stitched glove.

On the record it sounds as if the Strat is not just doubled but more interestingly I suspect this is the first high profile incidence of 'matchstick magic' – a matchstick jammed in the 3 position switch to wedge the contacts and give a combination of the

bridge and middle pickups. For more on this *see page 94* –
fitting a 5 position switch.

The guitars would have been miked with valve Neuman U47
or U48's or STC 4038 ribbon mikes into the EMI valve console
in Abbey Rd's studio 2, an environment virtually unchanged
from the days of The Shadows 'Apache'. Reverb would have
come from the same EMT plates or the classic 'echo room'. **NB**
See 'The Beatles Gear' by Andy Babuik for more on the precise
technical details.

The Strats remained in favour for 'Sgt Peppers Lonely Hearts
Club Band' and 'Magical Mystery Tour' – George remembered
using the Strat for 'I am the Walrus' – it is in fact seen in the
'Walrus' sequence of the film and again in the mega broadcast
of 'All You Need is Love'. By then George's guitar had acquired a
new self-administered psychedelic paint job, some of that
decoration being sourced from Pattie Boyd's green glitter nail
varnish. George christened the guitar 'Rocky' and adapted the
action for the slide guitar style he developed throughout his solo
career. It remains in the Harrison estate and was last seen at the
'Concert For George' at the Royal Albert Hall.

Jimi Hendrix

1968 Olympic White Stratocaster serial no 240981

On Monday morning, 18 August 1969, Jimi Marshall Hendrix took the stage at the Woodstock Festival and delivered a performance on his right-handed Stratocaster that began a new chapter in the history of the guitar.

Two minutes into Voodoo Chile he had already taken his Strat and its Marshall amplifiers to the known limit: the supreme showman, he was playing with his whole being – musician, performer, crowd pleaser. Then he took to the tremolo/vibrato in a way Leo Fender would never have dreamed of, 'divebombing' it to the limits of its capability to great musical effect.

After that he segued into The Star Spangled Banner. At first his delivery was relatively straight, and the predominantly American crowd – used to hearing their beloved anthem at football matches and ball games – cheered in recognition. But then Jimi took off on a sonic adventure, literally presenting a soundscape of the horror of the then-raging Vietnam War. Using a simple Fender Strat, he crafted his own 'Guernica', as sonically graphic as Picasso's infamous painting. The audience heard the screams of diving aircraft, the deadly machine-gun

rattle and the anguished howl of the dying. Helicopters churned over Woodstock, napalm burned, and The Last Post played. This was Hendrix's own 'Apocalypse Now'.

Jimi was an artist in sound and the master of an instrument that he personally reinvented.

■ Jimi's Woodstock gear

Jimi's year-old CBS Strat performed well, and the only concession to the extreme pressures he placed upon it was his frequent 'in flight' tuning. The divebombing adventures led to many imitative tributes, and eventually to the creation of the locking trem, locking machine heads, and other Floyd Rose innovations. (See the Mexican Strat case study on page 118.) The guitar was a stock off-the-shelf model with five trem springs in place pulling against his very light (for the time) Fender 'Rock'n'Roll' strings. Jimi had purchased it himself and kept it all his life. Following his death, Mitch Mitchell sold it via Sothebys, and in 1993 it was repurchased and passed to the Experience Music Project in Seattle.

To extend the Strat's sonic horizons in 1969, Jimi had relatively simple and purely analogue tools. Digital sound was 20 years in the future and undreamed of even by a Voodoo Chile.

His amp was a valve Marshall made in the UK, a '1959' JTM 100 Watt super lead with no master volume or channel switching, powered by three 12AX7 and four EL34 valves – the so called 'Plexi' amp. Behind him Jimi had 16 speakers in four Marshall cabs, which he likened to 'a couple of great refrigerators'.

Between the Strat and the amp were a few germanium transistor-powered analogue FXs. First in the circuit was a VOX Wah-Wah, the now familiar extreme tone control, adjusted at foot level by a simple potentiometer, the distinctive sound essential to the intro of Voodoo Chile. The small Fasel inductor coils in the Italian-made original were an important part of Jimi's distinctive tone.

This Wah-Wah pedal had apparently been accidentally developed in 1966 when a VOX engineer had been developing a new circuit for the Super Beatle amplifier. It is essentially a tone control activated by the player's foot. Rock the pedal forward and it produces a high-end, treble-heavy tone. Rock the pedal backward and it produces a tone that has a deeper, muted sound. Eric Barrett, Jimi's guitar tech and roadie, said at the time: 'Most people just touch it with their foot. Jimi jumps on it with his full weight, so I carry about three extra Wah-Wah pedals and ten extra fuzz boxes.' Though VOX were the first company to market such a device, its infinite tonal possibilities and electronic simplicity spawned armies of imitators.

Next Jimi had an Arbiter 'Fuzz Face', a primitive but effective mini amp, acting as a pre-amp stage to overload the Marshall's front end, generating a rich harmonic distortion. The germanium transistors were either two NK275s or AC128s. This detail was important, as was the matching of these wayward early transistors: a good, well-matched pair sounded terrific, but if poorly matched they sounded like a mistake.

The Fuzz Face was originally manufactured by Arbiter in 1966 to compete with other fuzz boxes of the day, such as the VOX Tone Bender. The Fuzz Face's distinctive round shape came about when the company's founder, Ivor Arbiter, spotted an old microphone-stand base and thought it would be a great shape for a stomp box. Hendrix employed the device almost as soon as it came out. However, because the sound of a fuzz box so closely resembles that of an overdriven amplifier, Jimi's use of the Fuzz Face is difficult to pin down.

The other FX on the Woodstock stage included a Univibe (an early four-stage phaser effect first developed in Japan by the Shin-Ei company): the second 'volume pedal'-like device seen in the film footage of Woodstock is part of this Univibe rig. A Merson musical products representative, quoted in Melody Maker on 11 September 1971, commented: 'We enjoyed a close relationship with Jimi, and our engineering staff developed a great deal of electronic gear for him. The Uni-Vibe is a device that simulated a rotating speaker sound with a wide-band variable speed control. It was initially designed for use with electronic organs, but was found to be quite adaptable for guitar. We gave one to Jimi, and he featured it prominently. We also gave him one of our Uni-drivers, which he had started to use before his tragic death.'

Jimi also often used Roger Mayer's 'Octavia', which electronically simulated a higher octave. This is best heard on the recorded version of Purple Haze. I can't see this on the Woodstock footage but it may possibly have been operated offstage. Built specifically for Jimi by UK electronics whiz Roger Mayer, and originally called the 'Octavio', this effect is an extraordinary combination of fuzz tone and simulated octave doubler. The Octavia (renamed by Mayer to differentiate between prototypes developed for Jimi and their commercially available counterparts) produces a sound that is an octave higher than the note being presently played, as well as creating some unique noises suitable for 'Wild Thing'.

■ Approaching Jimi's sound in the twenty-first century
In 2002, the Fender Custom Shop, under the direction of Mike Eldred, created four 'clones' of the guitar Hendrix used in his

historic Woodstock performance. Only one was made available for sale to the public. Of the other three, one was presented to the Hendrix family, another was presented to Seattle's Experience Music Project museum, and one was retained by Fender.

Jim Marshall now makes hand-soldered versions of his Marshall amps, completely identical to the original spec. They are expensive but good.

■ A sobering reminder
I have copies of Jimi's home demos. These consist simply of his Strat plugged into one channel of his quarter-inch tape 'reel to reel' Revox and a microphone plugged into the other. He still sounds good, and his Strat still sounds like a Strat played by Jimi Hendrix. We all need to think about that.

ABOVE Jimi and CBS Strat

Eric Clapton 2

'Blackie' – a hybrid Stratocaster put together from three different Strats, including 1957 serial no 20036

This famous Strat was Eric's main guitar between 1972 and 1987 and notably featured on the 1977 recording of 'Wonderful Tonight', which utilises the 'down the crack' neck and middle pickups for the famous lyrical solo. (*See page 94*)

In 1970, Eric bought six then unfashionable Strats for $100 each at the Sho-Bud guitar shop in Nashville, Tennessee. He took them back to England and gave one to Steve Winwood, another to George Harrison, and one to Pete Townshend. From the remaining three, he took the best components and assembled what became known as 'Blackie'.

Lee Dickson, Clapton's guitar technician of more than 26 years, says: 'Blackie is still around and 100 per cent playable, contrary to all rumours otherwise. It's the nature of those old Fenders that the neck can eventually loosen in the neck pocket, even with the bolts tightened. It had been refretted a couple of times and there was a lot of wear on the edge of the neck, which made it difficult to get E string vibrato easily. We tossed around the idea to have a new neck made for it, but eventually the decision was made to just retire Blackie.'

The guitar was eventually auctioned to raise funds for Eric's 'Crossroads' charity. David Belzer and fellow 'Burst Brother', Drew Berlin, representing Guitar Center Inc, successfully bid on 'Blackie' at Christie's 2004 Eric Clapton Crossroads Auction. It fetched nearly half a million dollars.

The detailed photographs show how much stress a guitar

can take on world tours over a period of more than 15 years. It's worth noting that though Eric is now using a Custom Shop Signature Strat, much of the work he is famous for has been produced on a totally 'stock' Strat with a rusty bridge and just five tensioned springs to provide his 'locked off' trem. The magic, it seems, is mostly in the imagination and inspiration of the player.

■ Eric's sound

In 1976, Clapton used modified Music Man amps (HD 130 Reverb) with the bias up all the way and special open-back cabinets.

Those who are interested in valve amplification may find the following of interest, but **NB**: This sort of adjustment should only be undertaken by a qualified electronics expert. Valve amplifiers can be lethal due to their 'hi tension' circuits. If in doubt, stay out!

'Biasing' an amplifier refers to setting the 'idle' current in the power output valves. All valves must be biased, both in the preamp and output stages. A valve is 'biased' by setting the amount of DC current that flows in the valve when there is no signal present at the valve's grid with respect to it's cathode. This DC bias current can be set in a number of ways. The bias point determines several things about a valve amplification stage. Increasing the bias has the effect of determining the power output, and the amount of distortion. The factors affected include:

■ The 'headroom' (being the size of input signal that can be applied before the output signal clips).

■ The efficiency of the stage (the amount of output signal power versus DC input power).

■ The gain of the amplification stage (the magnitude of the output signal for a given input signal).

■ The noise of the 'stage'.

■ The class of operation (class A, AB, etc). The proper bias point is always a trade-off or balance, and selecting the optimum bias point can be a difficult and skilled task best left to an expert.

Those who wish to know more are advised to consult the excellent Aiken Amplification website.

I assume Eric was having his guitar tech increase the bias on his amplifier valves to give a little more edge, perhaps a little more 'crunch', to his sound when he digs in and pushes the amplifier a little harder. This edge gives the sweet melody of 'Wonderful Tonight' a character all of its own and distinctly different to that same melody as it might be played by Hank Marvin or Mark Knopfler.

In the end what we are hearing is Eric's unique phrasing and timing, which give the solo his individual personality. Another technical factor in the sound of this recording is the discreet stereo delay and long reverb on the lead guitar applied by his engineer, probably at the request of the producer.

Mark Knopfler

1961 Vintage Stratocaster serial no 80470

This guitar is dated 1961, and refinished in red. The black volume knob seen in some photographs is naturally a replacement. In the 'Sultans of Swing' DVD the knob is simply missing. For many years it was quite hard to get hold of Fender replacement parts so you took what was on offer, black, white or even gold.

Another modification is the laminated maple fingerboard replacing the original rosewood. Mark was clearly aiming to emulate his hero Hank Marvin's 1958 maple neck Fiesta Red, though the paint job is somewhat darker and is now officially dubbed 'Hot Rod Red' for the Signature Mark Knopfler Strat.

The replacement fingerboard explains why the 1961 guitar has no 'skunk stripe' at the back of the neck and no dark spot at the headstock. The strap button is located rather unusually on the back of the guitar! These modifications were done by a repair-man called Sam Lee.

Mark Knopfler – The Sultan of swing

You can see this guitar in the 'Sultans of Swing' DVD, 'The Old Grey Whistle Test' DVD, and many photographs. It was Mark's main 'live' guitar for many years.

Clearly Mark's sound is unique and some of that uniqueness comes from his finger-style approach to the Strat. In July '79 Mark told *Guitar Player* magazine: 'I was into playing American music, especially the Blues. First, I learned how to finger-pick – just the basic stuff – and then I began developing a claw-hammer style. And all during this time I was playing my solid-body without an amp of my own … I used to use a pick until a few years ago, when I started getting more and more involved with playing without one. Then, a sort of synthesis happened between finger-picking and getting plectrum-type effects by just using my fingers. Eventually, I found myself doing things with just my thumb and two fingers that I couldn't do with a pick. But I still use a plectrum now and again for strumming or for playing on acoustic tracks.'

For 'Sultans of Swing' Mark plays with his thumb and first two fingers in a style reminiscent of his other hero, Chet Atkins. Interestingly Mark occasionally anchors his picking by putting his right-hand third finger on the fingerboard – this is faintly reminiscent of a 19th-century classical technique employed by players such as Carcassi.

'I carry two Fender Strats,' he said in the '80s. 'Both of them are '60s vintage: one has a maple neck, and the other is rosewood. On one there's a DiMarzio FS-1 pickup in the neck position for the bass, and I like it because it just seems to give a fatter, louder sound, with more clout than the standard pickup Fender uses. That's the only thing that isn't stock on either guitar … At the moment I'm using a Music Man [amp] with two 12in speakers.'

The unit referred to was a Music Man HD 130 (2 x 12in, 130W), which Mark used from 1978, the year 'Sultans' was issued. The HD 130 has a 12AX7 splitter tube in the otherwise solid state pre, feeding a power stage with four EL34s; two channels, one with tremolo and reverb; EQ on both channels; and a master volume control. There's a 'deep' and a 'bright' switch. No channel switching: it has a footpedal jack, which was probably to turn the reverb on/off. Its heavy transformers mean it weighs in at 45lb and usually came with black Tolex covering. It has a removable panel at the back, and a long heavy-gauge power cord. Power and standby switches are also on the back.

Mark used a Morley volume pedal, 'which I like because it's so dependable, and an MXR analogue delay, the little green box; I used it on the beginning of 'Down To The Water Line' … My playing is fairly straightforward, really, and everything's pretty much standard, no frills or special effects.'

In an interview in 1984 he offered some more details:

What does your picking technique consist of now?

'It's the thumb and first two fingers, and I tend to anchor with the back or my hand and my other two fingers, so it's a solid base.'

Do you pick with your fingernails or with the meat of your fingertips?

'It's really from skin, but sometimes the nail will catch. You can use the nail to snap it. A lot of times, I'll hit a note with the thumb and second finger together, so it might seem as though I'm pinching the string, squeezing it. The second finger hits it first I think, behind the thumb, so you can get a real physicality with a note.'

Your old Fender Strat used to have the three-way toggle switch taped so that it would stop in the position between the middle and rear pickups. Why didn't you just get a five-position switch to achieve the same pickup combination?

'I liked the three-way switch better than the five-position; it had a better sound. But I kept knocking it out. I have a five-position switch on the Strat now. The roadies are always pulling bits out and sticking things in.'

In '92 he told *Guitar Player*: 'It's a tremendous mistake to get involved in music theory and so on, and then discount things about playing because you just don't hear it, you don't see it, and it doesn't fit your formulas. I don't care how many jazz lessons you've taken, I don't care how many modal dingbats you know. This is all shit! You should have enough reverence for music to make your own education.

'I originally wrote 'Sultans of Swing' on my National steel guitar, open tuned. Same lyrics, but a different tune. Since I can't remember it, it was completely unremarkable! When I got the Strat and plugged into an old Vibrolux, it became something else.' (The reference is to a Fender Vibrolux of the early '60s, brown, one 12in speaker, about 30W. This could have been the amp used for the 'Sultans' session.)

Marks last word: 'It all comes down to this; what are you prepared to give of yourself?'

The 'Sultans' recording was produced by Muff Winwood and recorded, along with the whole first album, between 14 February–8 March 1978 at Basing Street Studios, London. The engineer was Rhett Davies, later to become a great record producer.

Currently Mark uses a range of Strats including a Sunburst '54. Fender have now built him a Knopfler Signature Strat. This has a comfort-contoured '57 lightweight ash body, Vintage-tinted '62 C-shaped maple neck, Texas Special single coil Strat pickups, an American Vintage vibrato, and, surprisingly, a rosewood fingerboard.

Jeff Beck

Jeff Beck vividly remembers his first Strat encounter:

'I saw one hanging in the window of a music shop in Charing Cross Road. I was with a guy from the Deltones – we'd skipped off school and got the bus up to Victoria. We didn't really care where we went – we just wanted to look around guitar shops. From the top of the bus I said, "I have seen the light!" and went bowling down the stairs, knocking the conductor out of the way, jumped off the bus and ran across the road. There was a sunburst Strat in the window and a blond Tele with an ebony fingerboard. I thought, "This is it!"

'We went in and the guy in the shop asked if we were interested in buying it. We said, "Y-y-y-yes!" We were 14 and he knew we didn't have the money but he let us play on it and it was like being on a cloud – we didn't come down for ages after.'

Jeff has gone on to become an avid collector:

'I've got one prize Fender that was given to me by the late Steve Marriott – a '53 or '54 Strat that looks like it should be in the V&A. It's got a seasoned ash sunburst body that has cracked due to age and it weighs a ton. It looks just like the Buddy Holly Strat. At some stage when I wasn't thinking too clearly – mid-tour, I think – I was getting a lot of feedback so someone kindly unloaded the original pickups and I don't know where they are. Another important Strat is a Surf Green "relic" signed by and nicknamed Little Richard.'

Jeff and his previous guitar tech Andy Roberts often experimented with different Strat necks. 'Jeff's got a lovely old 1960 mustard yellow Strat, but it's not the original neck,' said Andy. 'He'll change necks from one guitar to another to see if it performs any better – he usually does it to put on a thicker neck.

'When we went into the studio we'd take a selection of guitars and amps, but nine times out of ten he'd use a Jeff Beck Signature model and a Fender Twin Reverb, "The Twin". At that time, for gigs with The Playboys, he used a new Bassman and no effects – the man's like a walking effects unit anyway!'

According to Todd Krause of the Fender Custom Shop, who makes Jeff's personal guitars, there are currently three types of Jeff Beck Fender Stratocaster. The first forms part of the regular Fender Corona plant 'product line ten'. This represents a 'snapshot' of Jeff's favourite guitar and is updated approximately every ten years. The second Beck guitar is a 'Signature' guitar made by the Custom Shop team, updated perhaps every two to three years. The guitars Jeff currently plays himself are personally hand-crafted by Todd Krause in the Custom Shop and these are updated constantly as Jeff strives for perfection. As of July 2006

Jeff has just taken delivery of six new Olympic white master-built guitars.

Todd was kind enough to give me an interview:

Why six guitars?
'They are all essentially identical but some are spares and some are used for different tunings.'

What sort of neck is Jeff currently asking for?
'He currently favours a '60s style Oval or C neck, full but not fat.'

Are Jeff's guitars set up in any unique way?
'Yes Jeff's guitars are the most weirdly set up guitars I do. Particularly the trem is set very high at the rear – this gives Jeff a full step [a tone] of upward pitch on the first string. This fits Jeff's unique guitar style, which involves a lot of palm pressure on the trem for steel-guitar-like portamento effects. The trem has the common three-spring arrangement and Jeff has the trem backplate in situ to prevent the springs falling out! He only has a small amount of downward pitch change available due to the unusual trem angle.'

Does Jeff still use .011–.049 string gauges?
'Yes and no. He may start a tour using .009s and then move up to .12s as the tour progresses. This can cause problems with the Wilkinson nut, as this is really designed for .009s or .010s – higher gauges can cause binding, meaning the tech on tour can be forced to resort to dentistry tools to file a solution.'

Can you describe Jeff's current pickups?
'These are "noiseless" but single coil and slightly hot wound. They have steel slugs and magnets. They sound like a "warm" single coil not unlike Texas Specials.'

Are Jeff's stainless saddles similar to those on the American Series?
'They're slightly different, as they're machined not cast and made from a harder, denser metal.'

The current specification for the 'standard' Jeff Beck guitar features a soft C-shaped neck with a contoured heel for easier access to the higher registers. In addition it's 'wired' with Fender Special Design dual-coil ceramic Noiseless pickups and straight-ahead five-way switching.

■ Amplification

Despite his constant experimentation Jeff seems to have a special affection for the classic Marshall sound: 'The Marshall sound is the balls,' he says. 'It's the big daddy and it has that growl that no other amp has.'

In Jim Marshall's book *The Father of Loud* (2004) the following details are given for Jeff's Strat/Marshall stage rig:

Steve Prior, Jeff's current guitar tech, says that though Jeff still errs towards Marshall 50W heads his exact amplification and FX set-ups are in a state of constant evolution. This is what you'd expect from a unique guitarist who's moulded a very individual approach to guitar playing, taking the Strat to the limit.

■ One Jeff Beck Stage Rig

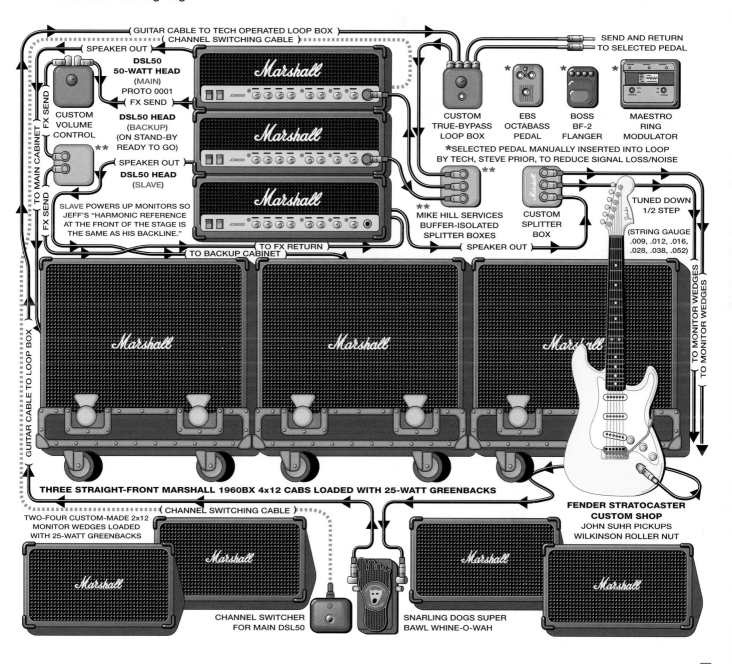

GUITAR CABLE TO TECH OPERATED LOOP BOX

CHANNEL SWITCHING CABLE

SEND AND RETURN TO SELECTED PEDAL

SPEAKER OUT

DSL50 50-WATT HEAD (MAIN) PROTO 0001

FX SEND

CUSTOM VOLUME CONTROL

DSL50 HEAD (BACKUP) (ON STAND-BY READY TO GO)

SPEAKER OUT

DSL50 HEAD (SLAVE)

SLAVE POWERS UP MONITORS SO JEFF'S "HARMONIC REFERENCE AT THE FRONT OF THE STAGE IS THE SAME AS HIS BACKLINE."

FX SEND

TO MAIN CABINET

FX SEND

GUITAR CABLE TO LOOP BOX

CUSTOM TRUE-BYPASS LOOP BOX

EBS OCTABASS PEDAL

BOSS BF-2 FLANGER

MAESTRO RING MODULATOR

*SELECTED PEDAL MANUALLY INSERTED INTO LOOP BY TECH, STEVE PRIOR, TO REDUCE SIGNAL LOSS/NOISE

MIKE HILL SERVICES BUFFER-ISOLATED SPLITTER BOXES

CUSTOM SPLITTER BOX

TUNED DOWN 1/2 STEP

(STRING GAUGE .009, .012, .016, .028, .038, .052)

TO FX RETURN

SPEAKER OUT

TO BACKUP CABINET

TO MONITOR WEDGES
TO MONITOR WEDGES

THREE STRAIGHT-FRONT MARSHALL 1960BX 4x12 CABS LOADED WITH 25-WATT GREENBACKS

FENDER STRATOCASTER CUSTOM SHOP JOHN SUHR PICKUPS WILKINSON ROLLER NUT

CHANNEL SWITCHING CABLE

TWO-FOUR CUSTOM-MADE 2x12 MONITOR WEDGES LOADED WITH 25-WATT GREENBACKS

CHANNEL SWITCHER FOR MAIN DSL50

SNARLING DOGS SUPER BAWL WHINE-O-WAH

Stevie Ray Vaughan

Hybrid Vintage Strat

As heard on 'Tin Pan Alley' Stevie Ray Vaughan and 'Number 1' – a rosewood 12in radius fingerboard 1963 (neck December '62) with retro-fitted left-hand trem block and gold-plated hardware. Serial number not known, and the guitar is currently missing.

'Tin Pan Alley' is one of Stevie's most subtle moments – the guitar virtually 'clean' throughout and with a very gentle phase effect, which may be one of his treasured Fender Vibraverbs, giving the illusion of a Leslie rotary speaker. The effect is enhanced by using two microphones on the speakers. These are panned half left and half right, giving the illusion of the Strat shifting gently across the soundstage.

The executive producer was the legendary John Hammond, and producer credits were given to the whole Double Trouble band. The engineers were Richard Mullen and Rob Eaton.

Stevie bought his favourite Strat second-hand in 1973. The 'bitsa' neck and body had 1959 'hot wound' pickups – that's to say, in common with many early Strats the pickups were inadvertently overwound by as much as 200 turns. The effect is replicated in the

Signature SRV guitar by the use of Fender 'Texas Specials': the SRV type have 600 windings per coil.

The original rather battered Strat had been refitted with gold hardware including a left-handed Vintage type tremolo/vibrato, jack socket, and tuners (Gotoh or Schaller type).

The neck had been re-fretted with Dunlop 6100 frets, and following numerous re-frets the fingerboard radius became rather eccentric, with the fingerboard becoming flatter nearer the body joint. Eventually the fingerboard had become so worn down that the neck was replaced with that from another of Stevie's Vintage guitars.

The best estimate gives SRV's guitar as a '59 Sunburst body with a '63 neck and a left-handed trem unit (Hendrix style).

Stevie liked to be able to dig in to achieve a weighty tone and would often use heavy gauge strings, sometimes as heavy as a .016 for a first! However, more often he used GHS – .013, .015, .019, .028, .038, .058, tuning down to E flat (down a semitone), a trick which he probably picked up from Jimi Hendrix. This gave his guitar a little more fluidity and less tension.

SRV used a range of tube amps for stage and studio, though the Fender Tweed Bassman 1959 predominated. Others included a Marshall JCM800 half-stack 100W (1962); Fender Twin 100W Dumble Steel String Slinger head with Dumble 4 x 12in cab; two 1964 Blackface Fender Vibroverbs with 15in speakers; Marshall Major 200W heads (Super lead and Super P.A.) with 8 x 12in and 4 x 15in cabs; Marshall Town & Country combo; Magnatone combo; Fender Harvard; Fender Vibratone rotating speaker cab; and Boogie Simu-Class.

The TS-808 Ibanez Tube Screamer was a crucial part of Stevie Ray Vaughan's tone. He used it to overdrive the front end of his tube amps and to add a natural tube-like saturation and sustain to his distinctive guitar voice. He used both the early TS-808 and the later TS-9 Ibanez Tube Screamer stomp boxes. The TS-808 is distinguished from the TS-9 by its small black knobs, smaller stomp button, white script on the housing, and darker green colour.

The SRV Signature Strat
Shortly before his untimely death in 1990, Stevie Ray Vaughan worked with Fender to produce a Signature Stratocaster guitar. It features an early '60s 'oval' neck shape, Pao Ferro fingerboard, Pao Ferro 12in radius (305mm) with 'jumbo' frets, three Fender Texas Special single coil pickups, gold-plated hardware, and an inverted left-hand vintage tremolo unit.

Eric Clapton 3

Signature Stratocaster

'While my Guitar gently weeps.'

No apologies for this return to the most well-known Stratocaster advocate. This latest incarnation of Eric's Signature guitar is one of three Fender Eric Clapton Signature guitars specially decorated by the New York artist 'Crash', who in an interview for the 'Strat Collector' website recalled:

'I first met Eric in New York when he was here for a big Grammy showcase. He was also in town to videotape street murals and other things for a project he was finishing. He wanted to know if anyone could show him around, show him the streets – some of the "underground" sites. Someone I know suggested me. He gave me a call.

'My name, Crash, came from my first year in high school. I was learning about business careers and chose computer programming as my major. "Crash" is a term for a computer breakdown, as we all know.'

John 'Crash' Matos was born in 1961 in the South Bronx, New York. With no formal art training he grew up on comics, graffiti, and cans of spray paint. His family are originally from Puerto Rico. His 'West Side Story' neighbourhood was one of young gangs, mostly Hispanic and Black:

'I was always aware of graffiti. Growing up in my 'hood, you noticed what's around you, and graff was the design. I started when I was 13, and the trains were the best place to get "showcased". I actually picked up doing graffiti from the older kids in my neighbourhood, guys like KAZOO143, CEN2 (RIP), EASE707, and others. They put my feet firmly in a place where I would eventually learn the art of spray painting.

'Eric had sort of asked me about doing something on a Fender back in '96 or '97, but with both of our schedules it was difficult. Then – one bright summer morning – I just had the urge to do one. I was able to contact Eric's guitar wiz, Lee Dickson, and he made arrangements with Fender to have an unfinished body flown to me.'

There have also been a limited number of 'Crash' Strats obtainable from the Fender custom shop (50 as we go to print). Eric commissioned eight other Graffitti guitars from other artists, so these too may turn up in concert eventually.

■ The guts of these guitars
Lee Dickson has the responsibility for maintaining Eric's Strats and keeping them in perfect working order throughout the most gruelling of world tours, concerts, and recordings.

Tellingly, Eric has no special set-up requirements – as Lee told me: 'Eric likes them straight as they come from the factory'. Needless to say a certain amount of special thought might go into how a Strat leaves the factory addressed to Eric Clapton!

The Strat retains the Vintage tremolo/vibrato but blocked off (see page 78) and uses old-style pressed steel bridge saddles– just like 'Blackie' and 'Brownie' before.

■ 29 November 2002, Royal Albert Hall, London

The gig Eric musically directed for his recently deceased friend George Harrison was a very personal farewell. Eric said in interview: 'I'm doing this for him but I'm really doing it for me'.

'While My Guitar Gently Weeps' had originally been recorded with Eric 34 years earlier for The Beatles' 'White Album', on 6 September 1968. For the ground track Paul McCartney played piano, Ringo drums, and George played rhythm guitar and sang the lead vocal. Paul later overdubbed the bass guitar.

Eric and The Beatles had met four years earlier in 1964 when Eric, then with The Yardbirds, was bottom of the bill at the Hammersmith Odeon and The Beatles were the headline. Eric gave George his first set of light gauge guitar strings in the days when such exotic delights were a rarity.

In 1968 Eric gave him the guitar to match, a Gibson Les Paul, the one he used on the 'Gently Weeps' session. Originally a Gold Top number 7-8789 from December 1957, the refinished wine-coloured guitar (nicknamed 'Lucy') had full-size PAF humbuckers.

The fact that 34 years later Eric used a Strat for the heart-rending 'Concert For George' version is, I think, very telling. Eric has clearly become used to the feel of a Strat and even when expected to play a Gibson, as for the recent Cream reunion, he still stayed with a Strat.

Looking back to the mid-'60s, Eric came to fame playing a Gibson Les Paul plugged into a Marshall 'Bluesbreaker'. This was his first 'signature' sound: he talked of 'woman tone' as that sound got louder and the tiny combo evolved into Marshall stacks and the Gibson guitars sometimes became 335s and SGs . But always humbuckers, with their fatter more middle frequency, emphasised sound. This also gave his amplifier more output to contend with, resulting in what Eric refers to as 'compression', a sometimes fairly subtle overload distortion.

His dramatic switch to Fenders and single coil pickups has worked well for Eric over the ensuing years. But somewhere deep inside I think he still sometimes pined for a bit more of that old Seth Lover 'crunch'.

With his current Stratocaster he has the best of both. The 'Vintage Noiseless' pickups are humbuckers! (see page 128) These stacked humbuckers combined with a 25dB MDX middle boost/treble roll off (and without the standard fitting TBX control which he prefers to disconnect on his stage guitars). Attached to an alder body at between 3.5 and 4.25lb and a classic maple neck, this gives Eric a guitar that looks like a Vintage '57 but can sonically pay tribute to his hero Buddy Guy one minute and is '60s Eric Clapton in the next. One physical difference is the flatter fingerboard radius – this makes Eric's signature tone plus bends sing without 'choking' as they would on a vintage Fender with a smaller radius.

When you see and hear Eric perform 'Gently Weeps' on the Concert for George DVD, it is clearly a very emotional event. Reunited on stage with Ringo and Paul McCartney, and with Danni Harrison looking like his dad's reincarnation, Eric plays and sings his heart out. From his supercharged Strat and a small Cornell Combo, Eric rings a personal and signature controlled grief – as he once reminded a fellow guitarist, 'It's While My Guitar Gently Weeps.'

As he builds his solo and that guitar gently pours out his loss, Eric gradually, and probably subconsciously, increases the gain on his MDX control. The sound resonates with his personal depth of feeling. For me it's a lifetime-best performance. Other guitarists may play faster, higher, and louder, but Eric reaches across the footlights and touches souls. For me that's what music is.

As Lee Dickson observes: 'People hear Eric's huge sound and they look on the floor – where are all the boxes? Where does it all come from? But that's just the way Eric plays. It comes from his heart and his brain, through the fingers and the Strat.

Eric Clapton and the TBX

Lee Dickson says: 'Eric likes to work with his tone controls flat out at 10, so the TBX control was ending up full on and sounding too 'zingy'. So we had Fender take them off his personal Strats, though they're still on the production models. Eric does use the MDX control, however.'

The TBX or Treble Bass Xpander control fitted to 'factory' Eric Clapton Strats looks like and works like a normal tone pot up to the centre detent. Beyond that it becomes an active EQ control. The TBX control is also fitted to some stock American Strats.

FENDER STRATOCASTER MANUAL

Appendices, glossary and contacts

Some further notes on guitar tuning, guitar materials, screw sizes and serial numbers.

LEFT Beautiful grained ash on a '54.

RIGHT A '54 – Ending as we began.

Understanding your Strat's materials

Technologically the Stratocaster was a child of its time, born of the American post-Second World War mood of optimism and regeneration.

The war had accelerated the development of thermoplastics, particularly for their use in aircraft. Leo Fender had followed this development and experimented with Bakelite, an early thermoset plastic developed by Leo Baekeland (1863–1944). Baekeland, a Belgian-born chemist, had discovered his thermoset plastic by accident in 1907. Bakelite was essentially a man-made liquid resin that wouldn't burn, boil, melt, or dissolve in any common acid or solvent. Once it was firmly set, it would never change. It was waterproof, had a high resistance to electricity, was impervious, and above all didn't melt.

However, Leo Fender wasn't that impressed with Bakelite and continued to make or commission many parts for his guitars from metal – for instance, the volume knobs on early Precision basses and Telecasters and the pickup cover in the Telecaster neck position. However, he was quick to seize on the potential of the newer thermoplastics. These, manufacturers claimed, could be moulded to any shape and were strong and electrically neutral.

Early plastics tended to disappoint, however. They were often unstable and consequently brittle, and the resultant fragments were sharp and dangerous. The present author spent his fifth birthday having an early plastic toy car removed from his knee, with five painful sutures to follow.

Several formulas were tried for the Stratocaster plastic parts before a satisfactory and durable solution was arrived at. A 1954 Stratocaster often has cracked or transparent pickup covers. However, Leo continued to experiment, as plastics suited his audacious instrument. The very shape of the Stratocaster is 'plastic' – a moulded comfortable and curved body.

Part of the genius of the Stratocaster is Leo's use of the best of traditional materials alongside the new. He employed metals for durability and resonance, wood for stability and 'feel', and the audacious new plastics for versatility and futuristic looks. Of the Stratocaster's approximately 150 parts (including strings and screws), approximately 107 are metal, two or three wood, and 15 plastic.

When the plastics buckled, as in the early single-ply pickguards, Leo applied a woodworker's traditional solution and made them three-ply. When the futuristic rounded pickup covers cracked, he recommissioned them with sharp corners.

A Mass-Produced, Disposable, Replaceable Future

By 1950 America's mighty automobile industry had set a pattern for the future. Everything, it seemed then, would soon be produced on the assembly line model. Every component was equal, perfect, and interchangeable.

Leo was caught up in this spirit, and though generally slow to automate he was quick to realise the benefits of the electric screwdriver for a guitar with about 45 screws holding it together. This is why the Stratocaster has Phillips screws, which are automated-screwdriver friendly (see page 48).

Tempered tuning – the great compromise

'Equal temperament' is the name given to a system of dividing the chromatic scale into 12 exactly equal half-steps. This is a compromise, but does allow us to play reasonably in tune in all keys and to modulate between keys during a performance.

Guitarists must learn to understand and accept equal temperament. (You might be interested to know that to approximate 'pure' chords in all forms would require about three dozen frets within the octave.) The system of equal temperament reduces the required fret number to twelve. A workable compromise.

Many guitarists are frustrated in their attempts to tune the guitar to pure chords (free of perceived 'beats'). These players have very sensitive ears that prefer 'pure' intervals and reject the mandatory equal temperament. They tune their guitar beautifully pure on one chord, only to discover that the next chord form is unacceptable. In too many instances they assume that there must be a flaw in the workmanship on the fingerboard. However, the problem is not in the construction of the guitar. Rather it is one of 'pure' or 'mean tone' tuning versus equal temperament.

A 'mean tone' fretted guitar would in fact only sound acceptably in tune in about three keys, so from the 18th century onwards we've learned to live with the compromise of equal temperament. Prior to this lutes and early guitars often had movable 'gut' frets which were tempered to the key of the piece to be performed. This system works fine until the piece modulates into a different key. The modern North Indian sitar still retains movable frets and the player tempers his frets according to the raga he is about to perform. Indian music, however, never modulates.

As practical working guitarists we must accept the equal tempered compromise, because the guitar is an instrument of fixed pitch and the strings must be tuned to tempered intervals, not 'pure'.

■ Appendix 3
Nut widths

The Strat started life in 1954 with a nut width of 1.641in, though hand-finished tolerances mean that early Strats have been found with nut widths of 1.685in. The '57 Reissue Strat has a width of 1.62in or 41.15mm, while the current American Series stands at 1.75in and the Chinese Standard Squier a narrower 41.46mm or 1.63in.

■ Appendix 4
Screw sizes

- Machine head: woodscrew – No. 3 x ⅜in round head Phillips – steel nickel plated.
- Scratchplate screws: woodscrew – No. 4 x ½in raised countersunk Phillips – steel nickel plated.
- Neck plate screws: No. 8 x 1 ¾in raised countersunk Philips – steel nickel plated.
- String guide screws: woodscrew – No. 3 x ⅜in Phillips round head
- Trem cover plate: No. 4 x ½in raised countersunk Phillips – steel nickel plated.
- Trem spring anchor: No. 8 x 1 ¾in raised countersunk Phillips – steel nickel plated.
- Jack plate: No. 4 x ½in raised countersunk Phillips – steel nickel plated.
- Strap button: woodscrew – No. 6 x 1in raised countersunk Phillips – steel nickel plated.
- Trem pivot: woodscrew – No. 6 x 1 ¼in roundhead Phillips – steel nickel plated.
- Octave screw: 4-40 UNC x ⅝in roundhead Phillips – steel nickel plated.
- Height adjustment 1 & 6: 4-40 UNC x 5⁄16in socket oval point – steel nickel plated.
- Height adjustment 2 to 4: 4-40 UNC x ⅜in socket oval point – steel nickel plated.
- Trem arm thread: 10-32 UNF.
- Truss rod: 10-32 UNC (some old truss rods were 8-32 UNC).
- Trem plate to block: 8-32 x ⅜in Phillips flat countersunk – steel nickel plated.
- Pickup screws: 6-32 UNC x ⅝in raised countersunk – steel nickel plated.
- Pickup selector: 6-32 UNC x ⅜in raised countersunk – steel nickel plated.

NB There are some variants notably the case study on *page 124*

■ Appendix 5
Pickup outputs

All figures relate to the bridge pickup with tone and volume out of circuit. I used an averaged sample of my own plectrum downstroke at the middle pickup position. All the guitars were amplified by the same Fender Hot Rod Deluxe, with the same volume and tone settings. The measurements were taken on a BBC spec Peak Programme Meter with peak hold. '0' level = .775V.

Comparative Pickup Outputs from the Case Study Guitars
Reference '0' level = –18dB.

- USA 1954 50th Anniversary Custom Shop limited edition –18dBV.
- USA American Standard 2005 –14dBV (NB: 4dB louder than the '54).
- USA Eric Clapton 2005 (active powered vintage Noiseless) –5dB (13dB louder than our ref!).
- USA Vintage Reissue '57 –16dB.
- Mexican Humbucker 2005 –8dB (10dB louder but subjectively still sounding very 'Fender').
- Chinese Affinity Squier –18dB (very in keeping with its Vintage vibe).
- Indonesian Squier –18dB (nice consistency here with the Affinity).
- Japan Fender 50th Anniversary –16dB (very similar to the '57 Reissue)

Subjective Comments
It was interesting to do this simple side by side test and I offer a few subjective comments as a guitarist:

- The '54 sounds very balanced, musical, and interesting, but it is still very punchy and bright. It must have scared the life out of the first Western Swing observers in 1954.
- The American Standard is rawer, more aggressive. Very 21st century.
- The Clapton sounds very powerful – just the thing for stadium filling. For me, however, some character is lost in the pursuit of signal to noise ratios. I think of the pickups as vintage 'decaffeinated'.
- The '57 Reissue sounds very balanced and has that classic slightly eccentric Strat sound. The pole pieces are set up for a wound third, which lends some unpredictability to proceedings.

- The Humbucker Strat is bright and surprisingly 'Fender-like', but with 10dB more potential for driving the front end of a Marshall amp.
- The Affinity Squier has a natural compressed Hendrix-like tone – and I have no idea why! Vintage output. I like its lightness.
- The Indonesian Squier sounds a bit bland but probably just needs a set of decent strings.
- The Japanese Strat sounds like a '60s rosewood fretboard to me – another classic sound.

■ Appendix 6
What is Agathis?

Squier Fenders made outside the USA are often made of a wood called Agathis. This is the name for a genus of giant tropical conifers found in rainforests in the tropical Far East and the South-West Pacific. The genus is a member of the Araucariaceae, the plant family that includes the Monkey-Puzzle and Cook Pine as well as the recently discovered Wollemi Pine, a botanical 'living fossil' from New South Wales, Australia. The Araucariaceae belong to the conifer group of plants, which also includes the pine family (pines, spruces, larches, firs, cedars), the podocarp family (podocarps, kahikatea, totara, etc), and the cypress family (swamp cypresses, giant sequoias, junipers, cypresses). Its timber is immensely useful and is increasingly being used in the manufacture of guitars.

■ Appendix 7
Fingerboard virtual radius

The original '54 Strats had a neck radius of approximately 7in, though this varied. In 1983 Elite and Standard Strats appeared with a radius sometimes as flat as 12in. A compromise 9.5in radius is common to many modern Strats, though Vintage Reissues tend towards a compromise of 7.25in.

■ Appendix 8
Neck profiles

The letters V, C, and U are used to describe the shape and contour of the back of the neck of Fender guitars. Necks described by these letters will correspond approximately to the shape of the corresponding letter of the alphabet.

The V-shaped necks come in 'soft' (fig 2) and 'hard' (fig 4) The 'soft' V shape is a bit rounded off, whereas the 'hard' V is more acute.

The letter C is used to describe two neck shapes, which *do not* have corresponding alphabetic letters – these are the 'oval' (fig 3) and the 'flat oval' (fig 5).

The U shape is usually clubby and rounded, with high shoulders (fig 1).

All this makes perfect sense when you put your hands on the various necks and get the feel of them.

There is sometimes confusion about the use of the letters V, C, and U to describe neck shapes and the use of the letters A, B, C, and D between the '60s and '70s to describe Fender neck widths at the nut. These letters stamped on the butt end of the neck had no relevance to the shape or contour these are references to nut widths. An 'A' neck was 1½in at the nut; B 1⅝in; C 1¾in; and D 1⅞in.

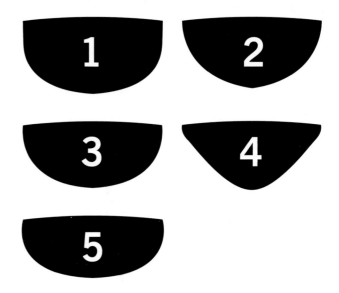

■ Appendix 9
Serial numbers

Odd serial numbers

AMXN + 6 DIGITS
California Series electric guitars '97 and '98

DN + 6 DIGITS
American Deluxe series instruments, '98 and '99

NC(XXXXXX)
Squier Strat Bullets (dating unclear)

FN(XXXXXX)
US made guitars and basses destined for the export market. Some may have stayed in the US or found their way back. (Made to Standard Strat specs, dating unclear)

I(XXXXXXX)
A limited number of these 'I' series guitars were made in '89 and '90. They were made for the export market and have Made in USA stamped on the heel of the neck

CN(XXXXXX), VN(XXXXXX)
Korean made Fender/Squier guitars (dating unclear)

CA(XXXXX)
Gold Strat 1981, '82 and '83

CC(XXXXX)
Walnut Strat 1981–82–83

GO(XXXXX)
Gold Strat 1982–83

SE(XXXXXX), SN(XXXXXX), SZ(XXXXX)
Signature Series Instruments

1988	SE8(XXXXX)
1989	SE9(XXXXX)
1990	SN0(XXXXX)
1991	SN1(XXXXX)
1992	SN2(XXXXX) etc
2000	SZ0(XXXXX)
2001	SZ1(XXXXX)
2002	SZ2(XXXXX) etc

3 DIGITS OF 500
35TH Anniversary Strat from 1989–1990

G(XXXXXX)
'STRAT' from about 1980,
(Gold hardware, 2 position rotary tone switch)

T(XXXXXX)
Tribute series instruments

C(XXXXXX)
Collectors Series

NB: As you can see neck dates are very important and a tally between these and the serial number is a good cross check. Neck dates are usually stamped or inked on the heel of the neck.

Please see Fender's own excellent website for more on serial numbers.

Year	Serial number
1950 to 1954	Up to 6000
1954 to 1956	Up to 10,000
1955 to 1956	10,000s
1957	10,000s to 20,000s
1958	20,000s to 30,000s
1959	30,000s to 40,000s
1960	40,000s to 50,000s
1961	50,000s to 70,000s
1962	60,000s to 90,000s
1963	80,000s to 90,000s
1963	90,000s up to L10,000s
1963	L10,000s up to L20,000s
1964	L20,000s up to L50,000s
1965	L50,000s up to L90,000s
1965	100,000s
1966 to 1967	100,000s to 200,000s
1968	200,000s
1969 to 1970	200,000s to 300,000s
1971 to 1972	300,000s
1973	300,000s to 500,000s
1974 to 1975	400,000s to 500,000s
1976	500,000s to 700,000s
	76 + 5 DIGITS
	S6 + 5 DIGITS
1977	S7 + 5 DIGITS
	S8 + 5 DIGITS
1978	S7 + 5 DIGITS
	S8 + 5 DIGITS
	S9 + 5 DIGITS
1979	S9 + 5 DIGITS
	E0 + 5 DIGITS
1980	S9 + 5 DIGITS
	E0 + 5 DIGITS
	E1 + 5 DIGITS
1981	S9 + 5 DIGITS
	E0 + 5 DIGITS
	E1 + 5 DIGITS
1982*	E1 + 5 DIGITS
	E2 + 5 DIGITS
	E3 + 5 DIGITS
	V + 4, 5 or 6 DIGITS
	(US Vintage Series
	except '52 Telecaster)
1983*	E2 + 5 DIGITS
	E3 + 5 DIGITS
	V + 4, 5 or 6 DIGITS
1984*	E3 + 5 DIGITS
	E4 + 5 DIGITS
	V + 4, 5 or 6 DIGITS
1985*	E3 + 5 DIGITS
	E4 + 5 DIGITS
	V + 4, 5 or 6 DIGITS
1986*	V + 4, 5 or 6 DIGITS
1987*	E4 + 5 DIGITS
	V + 4, 5 or 6 DIGITS
1988*	E4 + 5 DIGITS
	E8 + 5 DIGITS
	V + 4, 5 or 6 DIGITS
1989*	E8 + 5 DIGITS
	E9 + 5 DIGITS
	V + 5 or 6 DIGITS
1990*	E9 + 5 DIGITS
	N9 + 5 DIGITS
	N0 + 5 DIGITS
	V + 5 or 6 DIGITS

* For US Vintage Series, check neck date for specific year.

Year	Serial number
1991	N0 + 5 DIGITS
	N1 + 5 or 6 DIGITS
	V + 5 or 6 DIGITS
1992	N1 + 5 or 6 DIGITS
	N2 + 5 or 6 DIGITS
	V + 5 or 6 DIGITS
1993	N2 + 5 or 6 DIGITS
	N3 + 5 or 6 DIGITS
	V + 5 or 6 DIGITS
1994	N3 + 5 or 6 DIGITS
	N4 + 5 or 6 DIGITS
	V + 5 or 6 DIGITS
1995	N4 + 5 or 6 DIGITS
	N5 + 5 or 6 DIGITS
	V + 5 or 6 DIGITS
1996	N5 + 5 or 6 DIGITS
	N6 + 5 or 6 DIGITS
	V + 5 or 6 DIGITS
1997	N6 + 6 or 6 DIGITS
	N7 + 5 or 6 DIGITS
	V + 5 or 6 DIGITS
1998	N7 + 5 or 6 DIGITS
	N8 + 5 or 6 DIGITS
	V + 5 or 6 DIGITS
	(American Vintage Series)
1999	N8 + 5 or 6 DIGITS
	N9 + 5 or 6 DIGITS
	V + 5 or 6 DIGITS
	(American Vintage Series)
2000	N9 + 5 or 6 DIGITS
	Z0 + 5 or 6 DIGITS
	DZ0 + 5 or 6 DIGITS
	(Am. Deluxe)
	V + 5 or 6 DIGITS
	(American Vintage Series)
2001	Z0 + 5 or 6 DIGITS
	Z1 + 5 or 6 DIGITS
	DZ1 + 5 or 6 DIGITS
	(Am. Deluxe)
	V + 5 or 6 DIGITS
	(American Vintage Series)
2002	Z1 + 5 or 6 DIGITS
	Z2 + 5 or 6 DIGITS
	DZ2 + 5 or 6 DIGITS
	(Am. Deluxe)
	V + 5 or 6 DIGITS
	(American Vintage Series)
2003	Z2 + 5 or 6 DIGITS
	Z3 + 5 or 6 DIGITS
	DZ3 + 5 or 6 DIGITS
	(American Deluxe Series)
	V + 5 or 6 DIGITS
	(American Vintage Series)
2004	Z3 + 5 or 6 DIGITS
	Z4 + 5 or 6 DIGITS
	DZ4 + 5 or 6 DIGITS
	(Am. Deluxe)
	V + 5 or 6 DIGITS
	(American Vintage Series)
	XN4 + 4 Digits
2005	Z4 + 5 or 6 DIGITS
	Z5 + 5 or 6 DIGITS
	DZ5 + 5 or 6 DIGITS
	(Am. Deluxe)
	V + 5 or 6 DIGITS
	(American Vintage Series)
	XN5 + 4 Digits

Ashtray – Affectionate name for the original 1950's and 60's chrome bridge cover of a Fender Stratocaster, Fender Precision or Fender Telecaster. Often removed and lost.

Ball-end – Conventional type of guitar string end.

'Biasing' – Setting the idle current in the power output valves of an amplifier. A valve is 'biased' by setting the amount of DC current flowing through it when no signal is present at the valve's grid with respect to it's cathode. Increasing the bias determines the power output and the amount of distortion.

'Blocked off' – Term used to describe a tremolo/vibrato with a substantial wooden wedge behind the tremolo block.

Bullet-end – A patented Fender guitar string design that allows the string to travel freely in the bridge block channel during tremolo use and return afterwards to its original position in the bridge block.

Capo – abbreviation of 'Capodastro' originally a Spanish device A clamp across the strings of a guitar. Shortening the effective sounding length for musical transposition.

Dead spot – Spot in the machine head mechanism turn where no pitch-change is heard in the relevant string.

'Delta tone' pots – Potentiometers that provide no resistive load in the détente position.

Earth loop (or ground loop) – A situation that arises when two pieces of equipment with earthed mains plugs are also connected by audio cables effectively creating two paths to earth.

EQ – Equaliser.

Equal temperament – The name given to a system of dividing the chromatic scale into 12 exactly equal half-steps.

Feeler gauge – A gauge consisting of several thin blades, used to measure narrow spaces.

FX – Effects.

Gotoh – Manufacturer of bolt-on Vintage like machine head introduced in 1981.

Ground loop – See 'earth loop'.

'Hard tail' – Modification in which the bridge is screwed down hard to the body, or the tremolo/vibrato is 'blocked off'.

Heat sink – A means of drawing heat away from areas adjacent to components that are being soldered, often achieved by the use of crocodile clips or similar.

Humbucker – Double-coil pickups wired in opposite phase and arranged in parallel or stacked to cancel induced low frequency hum.

Kluson – Type of machine head used on early Stratocasters.

MDX – A mid boost circuit found on some Strats See Clapton Signature case study.

Micro-Tilt – Mechanism on some 70's and recent Fender guitars that uses an Allen key working against a plate to adjust the alignment of the neck.

'Nashville stringing' – Modification in which a banjo G string was substituted for a guitar's E first string, the E string subsequently used as a second string, the B string as its first unwound 'plain' third, the normal wound third as its fourth string, and so on.

N.O.S. – 'New old stock' a new guitar made as if of the model's original 'Vintage' year of manufacture.

PA – Public address system.

Pots – Potentiometers.

RF – Radio frequency.

Schaller – Type of machine head used on some modern Stratocasters.

Screen(ing) – Metallic shield around sensitive 'unbalanced' guitar circuits, connected to an earth potential to intercept and drain away interference.

'Skunk stripe' – Stripe of different coloured wood on the back of a Fender neck. It traditionally covered the truss rod when inserted from behind the fingerboard but is now sometimes purely cosmetic.

S.L.O. – A 'Strat-Like Object'.Every guitar manufacturer in the world seems to make one.

Superstrat – A modified Strat often with Humbuckers and or redesigned trem. See Mexican Strat case study.

'Swimming pool' – A large cavity beneath the pickguard to accommodate a range of pickups. Sometimes detrimental to the sound of the instrument and can also lead to body warping.

TBX – Treble Bass Xpander. An EQ circuit See Clapton Strat case study.

Wall warts – External DC power supplies.

Useful contacts

Guitars
■ The case study guitars were supplied by Peter Cook's Guitars, Hanwell, London (www.petercooks.co.uk), a good and knowledgeable shop with a long-established reputation.

■ The Japanese Strat was generously loaned by Lionel Coleman of London.

■ The Affinity Strat was provided by Ealing Music Services of London.

■ Tom Wood provided his Deluxe guitar.

■ The Deluxe switching was photographed at Patrick Reed Music, Kettering, England (www.patrickreedmusic.co.uk).

Specialist Tools and Parts
Stewmac in the USA (www.stewmac.com) has virtually every specialist tool and part you could possibly need to maintain and repair your guitar. UK contacts include www.axesrus.com, www.fender.co.uk, www.wdmusic.co.uk and www.allparts.uk.com.

Historic Guitar Information
www.backbeatuk.com – publishers of The Fender Book and many others.

Technical Advice
Fenders own website carries a range of useful drawings and schematics on most Stratocaster guitars – www.fender.com

Lemon Oil
D'Andrea, USA from www.musicexpert.com

Strings
www.djmmusic.com

Plectrums
www.jimdunlop.com

General Tools
Drapers – www.drapers.co.uk

Acknowledgements

My thanks to:
John Diggins, who understood the project and put up with my many questions. John makes very sophisticated guitars but understands the simple genius of the Strat.

The very patient guitar techs who answered my questions – Lee Dickson, Glen Saggers, and Andy Gibson.

Michael Leonard, editor of Guitarist Magazine, for advice and archive photographs.

Peter Cook's Guitar World, London, who made many of the featured Strats available: Trevor Newman, Paul White, Richard Scrace (who knows where the screws were on the scratchplate in 1960), Rob West, and Stuart Monks.

Draper tools for the generous supply of the general tools required.

Backbeat – Nigel Osborne and Tony Bacon for interest, enthusiasm, and a series of great books.

Judy Caine – without whom I would get nothing done.

Karl Balmer, who puts up with Daddy making a noise.

Brendan McCormack of Mind Scaffolding Inc, a constant source of inspiration and provocation.

Alex Perez and Todd Krause of the Fender Custom Shop.

Dave Gregory of XTC – for guitar advice.

The Jeff Beck interview with Douglas J. Noble was originally published in The Guitar Magazine volume 3 number 4, June 1993.

'The Guitar Player repair Guide' by Dan Erlewine.

The American Society of Luthiers.

Thanks to Fender, especially the guys in the Custom Shop and the excellent website.

Julian Ridgway at Redferns Music Picture Library for his help and instant response to requests.

Credits

Author – Paul Balmer
Editors – Louise McIntyre and Steve Rendle
Design – Richard Parsons and Lee Parsons
Copy editor – Ian Heath
Studio photography – Tom Wood, Carl Wilson and John Colley
Library photos – Redferns Music Picture Library

Index